Fast as the Wind
Contents

PART 1: Reading

THEME 1
The Danger Zone

THEME 2
Operation Wildlife

THEME 3
Yoshiko Uchida

THEME 4
Solutions, Inc.

THEME 5
Journey Into Space

THEME 6
Tales From Long Ago

THEME 7

To Be Continued . . .

Study Skills

PART 2: Language Arts

The Writing Center

Language and Usage Lessons

Capitalization, Punctuation, and Usage Guide

PART 1: READING

This Section Provides

- **Vocabulary, Comprehension, and Skills Support Pages for Major Selections**
- **Study Skills Pages for *Fast as the Wind***

Ghost of the Lagoon

Use the words in the box to complete the story below.

coral	vow	dorsal fin	phosphorescent
slay	vulnerable	reef	
lagoon	dismay	expedition	

The water in the ________________ was clear and shallow. Our guide said that at night, the light from the phosphorus in the sea grasses made the water shine with a ________________ glow. A long, narrow, L-shaped ________________ separated the lagoon from the ocean. We could see pieces of rough ________________ growing on the sides of the rocks. One of the rocks jutted up out of the water and looked like the ________________ of a shark! The guide said that the large opening in the reef made the lagoon ________________ to storms.

She told us that during one of these storms a pirate ship sank near here while on an ________________ to bury stolen treasure. According to legend, only the pirate king survived. He made a ________________ to recover the sunken treasure. Other pirates wanted the treasure and said that if the king were ever to recover it, they would ________________ him to get it. The king was so afraid and filled with ________________ that he never tried to find the treasure. Maybe it's still there, waiting to be found!

Ghost of the Lagoon

Look back at *Ghost of the Lagoon.* Think about the major events of the story. Complete the paragraph below to describe what happened.

When Mako learned that his father was killed by Tupa, he ____. Mako's mother needed more bananas, so Mako and his dog paddled ________ ____.
The sky was dark when Mako and Afa started home because Mako had also ____ __________. Suddenly Mako saw Tupa, which made him feel ____.
When Mako tried to balance the canoe, Afa ______________ ______________. Mako knew that he must spear Tupa before ____.
Mako wanted to be sure Tupa was dead because __________ ____.
Mako knew that when he returned home with the dead shark the villagers ____ ____ ____

The River of Ice

Read each sentence. Choose a word or phrase from the box that has almost the same meaning as the underlined word or words. Then write the word or words on the line.

numb	fugitives
Drinking Gourd	reality
efficiently	sympathizers
enslaved	uprooted

1. ______________ Before the Civil War, many African people were made slaves.

2. ______________ These people were removed from their homes in Africa and shipped to America.

3. ______________ Slave owners often beat their slaves in order to force them to work without wasting time.

4. ______________ Though many slaves dreamed of being happy and free, their facial expressions showed that the truth of their situation was often unbearable.

5. ______________ Many activists helped slaves who were escaping.

6. ______________ They hoped to gain the support of those who felt the same way throughout the country.

7. ______________ Escaping slaves would most often travel by night, following the group of stars that points north.

8. ______________ The hands and feet of slaves escaping during winter often became cold and lacking in the ability to feel or move.

The River of Ice

Think about the major events in *The River of Ice*. Then complete the sentences below. When the sentences are complete, show the order in which they occurred by writing the correct number in front of each. The first sentence has been done for you.

[1] Eliza decides she must try to escape because **she learns she will be sold and will be separated from Caroline, her daughter.**

[ ] After Caroline is pulled from the ice, Eliza ______

[ ] When the freezing water begins to cover Caroline, Eliza ______

[ ] When Eliza arrives at the river, she decides not to cross it because ______

[ ] Searching for a place to rest while she waits for the river to freeze, Eliza ______

[ ] The night after they cross the river, Eliza and her daughter ______

[ ] When George tells Eliza that slave hunters are searching for her, Eliza ______

Rising Action, Climax, Falling Action, and Sequence of Events

You have learned about the importance of the sequence of events in a suspense story. You have also learned to identify which of these events belong to the rising action, climax, and falling action. Look for these story elements as you read "Summer Storm."

Summer Storm

"Emerald Lake, 3.2 miles," Max's little sister Dana read the trail marker aloud.

"We're almost back at the campsite," said Max. They had climbed so high that they had passed the timberline — there were no trees, only rocks, moss, and tiny wildflowers.

The weather that morning had been perfect for a mountain hike. When Max and his sister had set out, though, their father had told them to be back by two o'clock. He had heard a weather report warning that a storm was coming. Max had promised to return on time, but he hadn't counted on Dana running ahead and wandering off the trail. It had taken him almost an hour to find her. He glanced down at his watch and noticed that it was 3:30. He knew that he'd have a lot of explaining to do.

But the suddenly darkened sky worried him more. The clouds had turned a dark gray, and the wind was picking up. It tore across the side of the mountain, throwing sand and dirt. A white flash of lightning pierced the air, followed by an ear-splitting clap of thunder.

"Max!"

"It's the storm Dad warned us about! We have to get off the mountaintop before it hits."

As Max and Dana ran across the mountaintop the sky grew darker and the air turned very cold. Then hailstones began to fall, hitting Max's face and arms with stinging force.

Max knew how dangerous lightning could be. Up there above the timberline there were no trees, and lightning usually struck the highest thing around — including people. "We need to find shelter," Max gasped.

"Where . . . where can we go?"

"Just run as fast as you can!"

They sprinted across the trail.

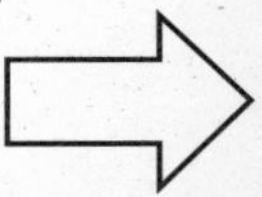

More flashes of lightning were followed by louder thunderclaps. Suddenly Dana grabbed Max's coat.

"I'm slipping, Max!" she screamed. Before either of them knew it, they tumbled thirty feet down the side of the mountain and slid into a ditch.

"Are you okay, Dana?"

"Just a few scratches."

Max realized that they had accidentally found a great shelter from the lightning. He lay down beside his sister and held her hand.

When the storm ended, Max and Dana heard their parents' scared voices shouting for them. The children answered, "Here we are! We're fine! We're fine!"

Max and Dana climbed out of the ditch. They hugged their parents and cried with relief before they all headed back down the trail to Emerald Lake.

Complete the chart below by writing two events from the rising action, one event from the climax, and two events from the falling action. Write the events in the correct sequence.

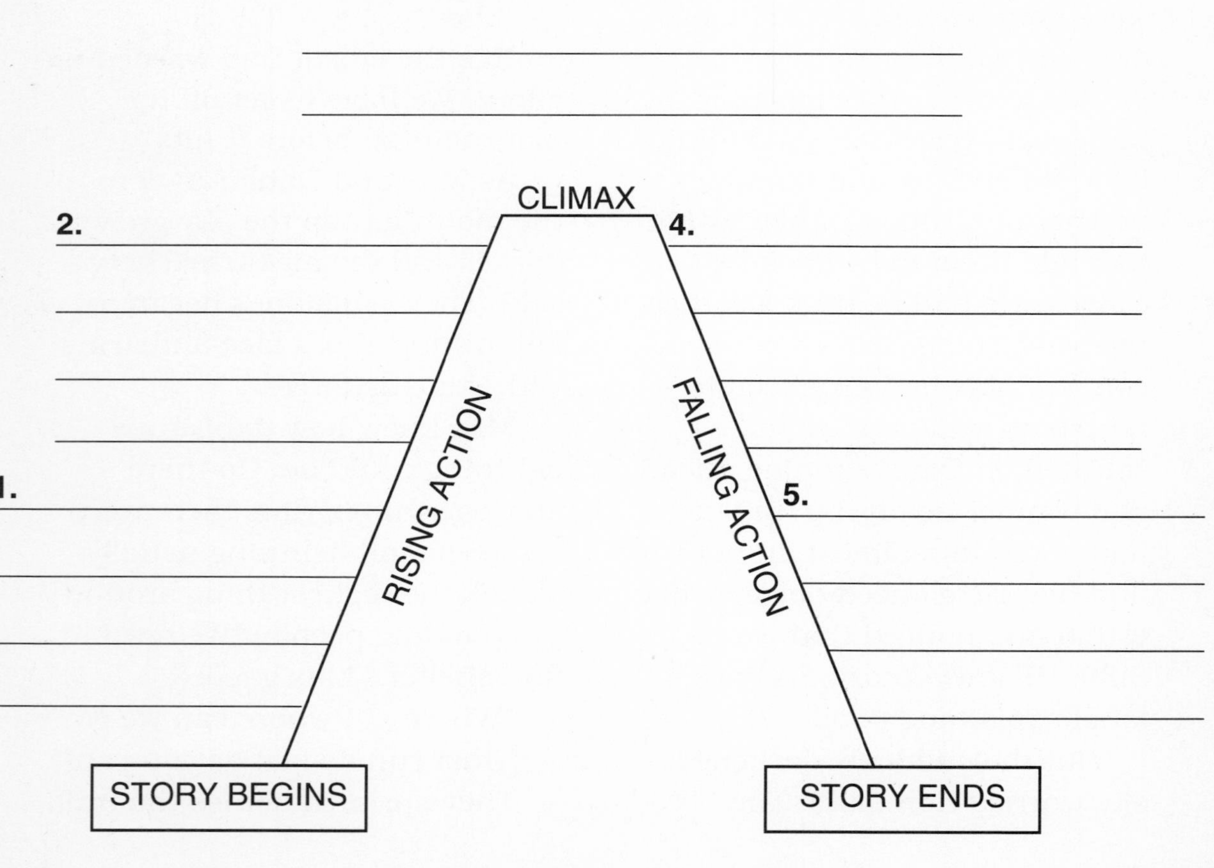

Where's Buddy?

Use the words in the box to complete the story.

suffocating	reaction	exertion
drained	insulin	smothered
syringes		

Gina liked to explore the mountain behind the farm with her grandmother. Because of Gina's diabetes, they always took a medicine bag that contained her ________________ and ________________ so that Gina could give herself a shot later in the afternoon. A diabetic ________________ up there on the mountain would be dangerous. But Gina knew that she would have her medicine bag, so she didn't need to panic.

One day they set out on a hike. It took a lot of ________________ to climb the steep trail, and by lunchtime, they both felt ________________. They rested on a big flat rock and ate. After lunch, Gina walked up the path to explore a cave her grandmother had found years before. When Gina came back, she stretched out on the rock. "The cave was too cramped," Gina said. "I couldn't breathe. I felt as if I were ________________. Why be ________________ by cave walls when there's all this beautiful open space to enjoy!"

Where's Buddy?

Look back at the story *Where's Buddy?* Read each problem from the story. Write how the story characters solved the problem.

PROBLEM	SOLUTION
1. Mike was in charge of looking after Buddy and making sure he took his insulin shot, but Buddy was missing.	**1.**
2. Mike thought Buddy might be in the cave, but he hated the idea of crawling into it again. Cramped spaces made Mike panic.	**2.**
3. The tunnel was too narrow for Mike because he'd grown since the last time he had explored the cave.	**3.**
4. Buddy had had a reaction and was unconscious when Mike found him.	**4.**
5. Seawater was filling the tunnel of the cave.	**5.**
6. Mike and Buddy knew their mom and dad would be very angry with them.	**6.**

Andy Bear

Use the words in the box to complete the article that follows.

habits	unpredictable	captivity	pacifiers	Arctic
habitat	digestive system	formula	incubator	clinic

Animal Oddities

All animals have their own __________________, or ways of behaving. When horned toads become frightened, they squirt blood out of their eyes. Horned toads live in the desert. They need a dry __________________ in order to live.

Lemmings need a cold place to live. Many lemmings live in the __________________. Lemmings have been known to march to the ocean and throw themselves in. No one can tell when they will do this. They are very __________________ animals.

Penguins live in the Antarctic. Eggs laid by penguins living in __________________ in a zoo are often kept in an __________________ to keep them warm. Adult penguins feed their young in an unusual way. The __________________ of a baby penguin can't handle solid food, so the parents eat the food first and then cough it back up for their baby. When human babies are hungry, parents often feed them __________________. When they cry and fuss, __________________ are often used to calm them. When they are sick, they are taken to a __________________. Penguin babies in the wild don't have baby bottles, formula, or clinics — and they're on their own when they turn six months old.

Andy Bear

If you need help with these words, look in the glossary: captivity, digestive system, habitat, incubator.

Before You Read What might you learn by reading the selection? Reread what you wrote on Journal page 33. Keep your prediction in mind as you read.

Read page 77. Then answer the two questions below.

1. Why are polar bears in danger?

____

____

2. Why is Constance Noble's work so important?

____

____

____

Read page 78 through the second paragraph on page 83. After you read, fill out the chart below.

Andy's Vital Statistics

Bear's full name ______________________ (page 82)

Date of birth ____________ Place of birth ____________ (page 82)

Weight at birth ______________________ (page 82)

Father's name __________ Father's weight ____________ (page 78)

Mother's name __________ Mother's weight ____________ (page 79)

Read through page 85. Then complete the sentences that follow.

Andy's Early Life

Three Days Old

By the time Andy is three days old, his appearance changes.

His pink nose and foot pads ______________________.

One Week Old

Andy weighs ________________ by the time he is one week old.

Twenty-eight Days Old

Andy looks different. He ________________ for the first time.

His fur is ____.

Four Weeks Through Eight Weeks Old

Andy gets sick because he ________________________________.

Constance worries about Andy's survival because he only

weighs ________________.

Read to the end of the selection. Then come back and complete the sentences below.

Two Months Old

Andy is feeling much better. Constance can tell Andy is feeling

better because he ________________________________.

Three Months Old

Andy plays in the snow. He isn't cold because ________________

____.

Four Months Old

It's time for Andy to return to the zoo. He now weighs ________________.

His claws are ________________, and his teeth

are ________________.

After You Read Use what you learned about polar bears and their way of life to write about another problem Andy might face in adapting to life in the zoo.

____

____

____

____

Andy Bear

Look back at *Andy Bear: A Polar Cub Grows Up at the Zoo.* Decide whether each statement below is true or false, and circle that answer. Then write a reason for your answer. The first one has been done for you.

1. The polar bear habitat is in danger. (True) False

   The search for oil and minerals in the Arctic threatens to destroy the polar bear's environment.

2. In the Arctic, mother polar bears and their newborn cubs live in dens and are safe from male bears. True False

3. Raising polar bears in captivity is easy. True False

4. Constance was able to think fast and save Andy from Thor. True False

5. Finding the right formula for Andy to eat was a big problem. True False

6. Constance was alarmed when Andy's pink nose and foot pads started to turn black. True False

7. Andy turned out to be the perfect pet. True False

Sterling

Use the words in the box to complete the story that follows.

exercise	specialists	recovering	orphaned
reflexes	rehabilitation	abandoned	tempt

Lin and his sister had been watching a little bird. It hadn't moved for two hours. Lin wondered if its mother had __________________ it. Maybe something had happened to the mother bird. Maybe the little bird needed help because it was now __________________.

The children wondered what to do. The little bird tried to hop away when they went near it. That made Lin think its __________________ were all right. Earlier Lin had put a bit of meat near the bird to __________________ it to eat. But the bird hadn't touched the meat.

Lin decided to call the zoo and talk to one of the zoo's __________________ in bird behavior. The woman Lin talked to said the bird was probably very young and was just learning to fly. The bird might be tired after getting so much __________________. Or possibly it was __________________ from a rough landing and was in need of some rest. The woman suggested leaving the bird alone for a while. "Let it have its own period of __________________," she said. "Call me this afternoon if it is still there."

As Lin hung up, his sister came in. "It's all right now," she said. "All of a sudden it hopped and flew off!"

Sterling

Look back at the selection. Write an answer to each question, using information from the selection.

1. What is the most common type of seal found in New England?

2. How did the Marine Mammal Stranding coordinator decide that the seal pup had been abandoned?

3. How was Sterling fed at the New England Aquarium?

4. Why was it important for the young seal pups to get exercise?

5. Why was it important to help the seal pups learn how to fish and become independent?

6. By the time the seal pups were two months old, how had they changed?

7. Why did the keepers want to return the seal pups to the wild?

8. What dangers do harbor seals face in the wild?

9. What should be done to help seals?

Main Ideas, Supporting Details, and Author's Point of View

Read the passage below. Decide what the main idea is, and look for details that tell more about the main idea. Then follow the directions after the passage.

The Mystery of the "Sleeping" Sharks

"I've just found a cave full of dead sharks!" thought Carlos Garcia, a young fisherman from the Mexican coast. It's no wonder this was his first thought on seeing the sharks. The sharks weren't acting like any he'd ever seen. These just floated as if they were sleeping or dead. What were these fierce sharks doing hiding in an underwater cave?

Ramon Bravo, one of Mexico's top underwater naturalists, came to the cave to see the sharks. After he dived into the cave to get a closer look, he agreed: the sharks were behaving strangely. Bravo recognized them as requiem sharks. Requiem sharks are usually quick-moving and dangerous. If they see something move, they will either flee or charge toward it. But these sharks didn't even seem to notice that he was there.

Bravo got in touch with his old friend Eugenie Clark, a scientist nicknamed the Shark Lady. After Bravo told Clark about the unusual sharks, she decided to have a look for herself.

Studying the "sleeping" sharks turned out to be a long, difficult job. Day after day, Clark and her crew worked to find out why the sharks were acting so unusually. Part of this work involved learning about the waters inside the cave. The scientists measured how deep and cold the water was and how fast it moved. They did tests to find out how much oxygen and salt was in the water. They spent hours underwater, watching the sharks. Because the sharks weren't really sleeping, the job could be dangerous. A wrong move could make a shark come to life. So they learned to move cautiously as they scribbled notes on clipboards and took photographs and movies.

After studying the results of her experiments, Clark discovered that fresh water from the mainland was seeping into the cave and mixing with the seawater. Perhaps the sharks

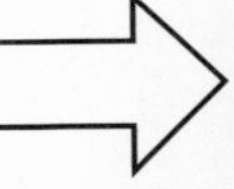

were attracted to the cave by this fresh water?

Clark came up with this theory when she noticed something important. The sharks inside the cave had very few parasites living on them. Parasites are small animals that attach themselves to larger animals and live off them. Clark remembered that parasites loosen their hold in less salty water.

One of Clark's students, Michael Resio, also pointed out that this sudden mix of fresh and salty water might affect the sharks' brains and perhaps calm them.

Clark decided that it was possible that the sharks came to the cave to get rid of their parasites. Then they remained there "sleeping" to enjoy the calming effects of the waters. She knew that more study was needed to prove this theory. Still, she felt she had made a good start at solving the mystery of the "sleeping" sharks.

1. Read the sentences below. Decide which sentence best tells the main idea of *The Mystery of the "Sleeping" Sharks*. Then draw a check mark in the box in front of the sentence.

☐ Eugenie Clark was nicknamed the Shark Lady because of her work with sharks.

☐ After much study, scientists think that sharks may swim into the underwater cave to get rid of their parasites.

☐ Scientists tried many different ways of testing the waters of the underwater cave.

2. Supporting details tell more about the main idea. Look back at the passage. Find two supporting details and write them here.

____

____

____

3. What do you think is the author's point of view? Use details from the story to help you explain how the author feels about Ramon Bravo, Eugenie Clark, and the other researchers.

____

____

____

____

Turtle Watch

Use the words in the box to complete the diving report below.

verge	emerge	oceanographers
barnacles	prod	upheaval
instinctively	predators	secreting

Diving Report

Date: June 16 **Location:** the Red Sea

Today I went diving in the Red Sea. My goal was to study the sharp ________________ that attach themselves to undersea rocks. These sea animals attach themselves by ________________ a liquid that is as sticky as glue.

Three other ________________ and a conservationist joined me on the dive. As we swam, we approached a school of silver-colored fish. Fearing that we were ________________, the fish ________________ swam away.

Soon we found an underwater cliff. Using special tools to ________________ the barnacles and pry them off the cliff, I accidentally knocked a large boulder off its rocky ledge. All around us rocks began to fall. It looked like the entire cliff was falling to the ocean floor below. During all this ________________, a rock hit one of the divers and dragged him to the ocean floor. He was on the ________________ of being covered by boulders when I rescued him. As we swam to the surface, I couldn't wait to ________________ from the water and carry the diver safely to shore.

Turtle Watch

Each statement below is a main idea from *Turtle Watch*. Read each statement. Then write two details that support it.

1. Sea turtles are endangered because of the products humans make from them.

Detail: ______________________________

____

Detail: ______________________________

2. Sea turtles lay their eggs in the sand on the shore.

Detail: ______________________________

____

Detail: ______________________________

____

3. The TAMAR scientists protect the turtle eggs until they hatch.

Detail: ______________________________

____

Detail: ______________________________

____

4. Rosa and Flavio help the scientists save the turtles.

Detail: ______________________________

____

Detail: ______________________________

____

5. Baby turtles must travel to safety after they hatch.

Detail: ______________________________

____

Detail: ______________________________

____

The Best Bad Thing, Part 1

Demonstrate your understanding of the underlined words by completing the sentences below.

1. The forlorn sound of the train whistle made me feel ______

______

2. Facing the principal after the accident was a tribulation for me because ______

______

3. When the doctor said that it was vitally necessary to take the medicine, she meant ______

______

4. When my father asked me to help with the dinner, I decided to oblige him by ______

______

5. The deep-sea diver became desperate when she saw ______

______

6. When the clerk told the woman how much her groceries cost, the woman became flabbergasted because she ______

______

7. The baseball team showed their gumption and moxie when they ______

8. Cleaning each window in the large house was a trial because

______

9. I knew the man was eccentric when he ______

______

The Best Bad Thing, Part 2

Use words from the box to complete the sentences.

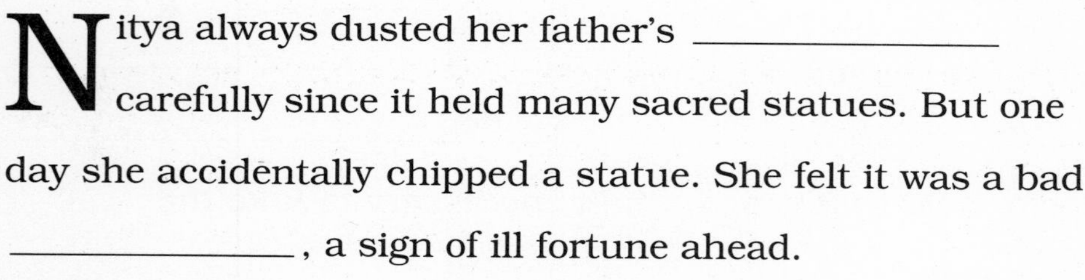

philosophical	influenced	omen
meek	thermal	ornery
shrine	stern	

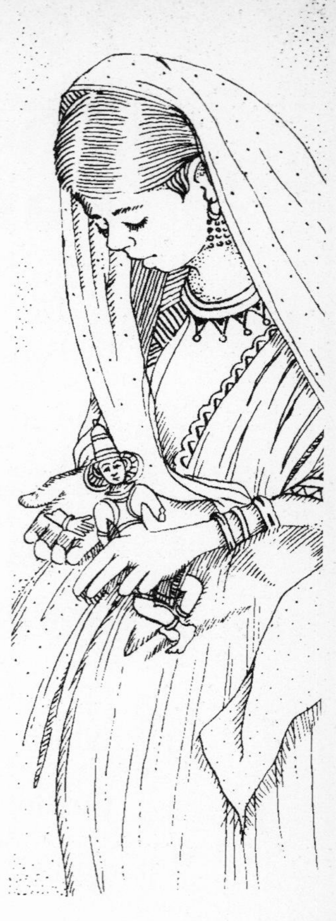

Nitya always dusted her father's ______________ carefully since it held many sacred statues. But one day she accidentally chipped a statue. She felt it was a bad ______________, a sign of ill fortune ahead.

Once before, when Nitya was very young, she had broken another statue. She had been behaving in an ____________ way and had thrown a toy at the shrine. Nitya's father had been very angry. Knowing how upset her father would be now, Nitya was terrified to tell him the bad news.

Later that day Nitya overcame her fear and told her father about the statue. With a ______________, apologetic voice, Nitya explained what had happened. As she told her father about the statue, his face had a very ______________ look. But to Nitya's surprise, her father was not angry. Instead, he explained in a ______________ way that trust and honesty are more important than objects. Nitya knew her father's love for her had ______________ the way he reacted. He suggested that they forget about the statue and enjoy the sunny weather by flying kites. Because there was a ______________ that day, Nitya's kite flew very high.

The Best Bad Thing, Part 3

Read the story and think about the meaning of each underlined word. Then write the word next to its meaning below.

When Yin heard the discouraging news about her aunt's accident, Yin decided to see her as soon as she could. On the way to the hospital, Yin bought a bouquet of daisies. Daisies were her aunt's favorite flower and Yin hoped they would cheer her up.

After seeing her aunt at the hospital, Yin decided that her aunt did not look as pathetic and weak as she had feared. The blood transfusion seemed to have picked up the woman's spirits as well as speeded her recovery.

Later, when Yin talked to the doctor, he said he had only a vague idea of when her aunt could come home. He wasn't sure when she would be well enough to leave the hospital.

	Words	**Meanings**
1.	______________	not clear or distinct
2.	______________	causing one to feel pity or sympathy
3.	______________	the putting of blood, plasma, or other liquid into a person's bloodstream
4.	______________	depressing, disheartening

The Best Bad Thing, Part 4

Read each sentence and pay attention to the underlined words. Choose a word from the box that is similar to the underlined words. Then write the word on the line.

facilities	betray	seances
deported	notions	adequate
revelation	immigrants	intact

1. ________________ Jason's grandparents were newcomers to the United States.

2. ________________ They joined the rest of their family in America because they wished to keep their family together.

3. ________________ They became United States citizens, so they weren't afraid of being sent back.

4. ________________ To help immigrants face their problems with dignity, Jason's grandparents often volunteered at the city's immigration buildings.

5. ________________ Jason's grandparents helped immigrants find satisfactory places to live.

6. ________________ Jason liked to ride in his grandparents' old sports coupe and listen to stories about meetings where people try to contact spirits.

7. ________________ His grandmother used a secret recipe to make cookies. Jason promised not to be disloyal to her by telling anyone the recipe.

8. ________________ Jason liked to listen as his grandfather shared many of his ideas about nature.

9. ________________ When Jason grew up, he had a sudden realization that those enlightening talks had helped him decide to study plants and animals.

The Best Bad Thing

Think about what caused the events of the novel to unfold. Then complete the cause-effect chart below.

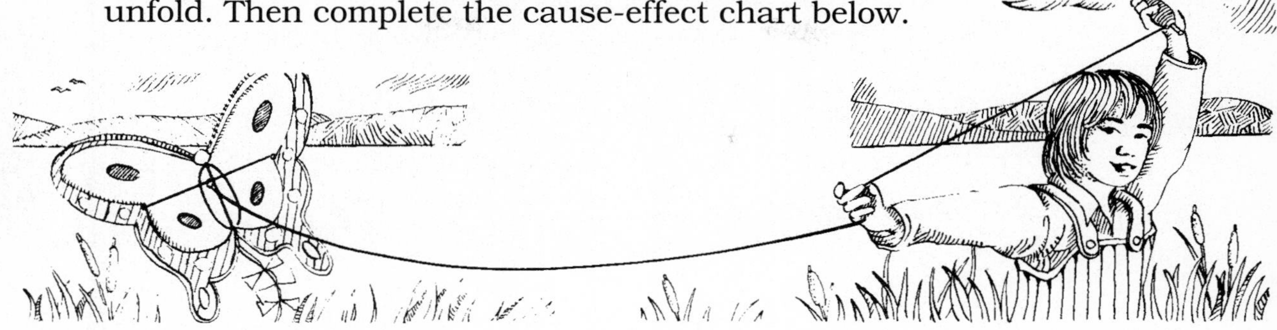

Cause		Effect
Mrs. Hata needs someone to help work in the fields and look after Zenny and Abu.	→	
Zenny tells Rinko about a freight train that jumped the tracks and tore up a lot of railroad ties.	→	
The old man sees a big man threaten Zenny, Abu, and Rinko as they are gathering the railroad ties.	→	
Rinko rides the freight train and jumps off.	→	
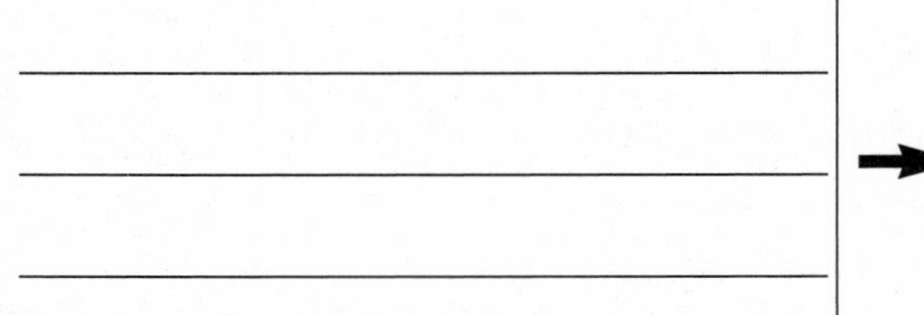	→	Rinko, Zenny, and Abu enter the barn and see the old man painting a samurai face on a kite.

Cause	Effect
______________	Mrs. Hata, Rinko, and Zenny take Abu to the hospital.
Mrs. Hata leaves the keys in the truck.	______________
Mrs. Saunders visits the Hata farm and asks questions about how Mrs. Hata can afford food and clothes for Abu and Zenny.	______________
______________	The old man decides to go back to Japan.
Mrs. Saunders misunderstands Mrs. Hata and thinks that she has made plans to marry a man who can support a family.	______________
______________	Mrs. Hata is able to stay on the farm and support her family.

Inferring Characters' Feelings, Actions, and Motivations

Read the story. As you read, think about the characters' actions, feelings, and motivations. Also think about the cultural details the author includes in the story. Then answer the questions that follow.

The River of Memories

"Tomas!" called Alberto Gonzalez to his older brother. "Could you take my friend Chhak and me to the library?"

Tomas had just come home from his job at the cannery. He was exhausted but he agreed.

At the library, Alberto told Tomas, "Chhak is from a village in Cambodia, near a river called the Mekong. It's a beautiful river with blue-green water. He feels sad when he talks to me about his village and the Mekong, so I thought that if we found a beautiful river here, it would help him feel at home."

"That's a good idea," said Tomas, "but there isn't such a river in Oakland."

"But there are beautiful rivers in other parts of California," the librarian assured them, as she handed them an atlas.

Alberto and Chhak turned to the back of the atlas where there were photographs of California. When Chhak saw a picture of the Sacramento River his eyes lit up. They had found what they were looking for. Now all they had to do was find a way to get there.

At suppertime, the brothers told their parents about their idea. Mr. Gonzalez called his friend Mr. Biari, a fisherman. Mr. Biari said that he had a friend who owned a boat on the Sacramento. He promised to call and make all the necessary arrangements for a boat ride.

Alberto and his parents went to see Chhak and his family the next evening. Mrs. Phot served a delicious meal made of vegetables, garlic, and pork wrapped in a kind of small rice pancake.

Mr. and Mrs. Phot couldn't speak English very well yet, but they were going to school to learn. Chhak and his sister, Somsimen, helped them when they had trouble. With Chhak's help, Mrs. Gonzalez explained the reason for the visit. Though they had difficulty understanding Mrs. Gonzalez, Mr. and Mrs. Phot accepted the invitation to take a boat ride.

Finally the day of the trip arrived. Mr. Biari's friend, Mr. Martino, was waiting for them at the river. They boarded the boat and began the trip downstream. All afternoon, as they floated down the river, they sang songs. Mr. and Mrs. Phot didn't know the words to any of the songs, so they taught the others a Cambodian song. It took quite a while for Mr. Martino and the Gonzalez family to learn how to pronounce each word of the song. Then Mrs. Phot hummed a tune from a traditional Cambodian dance called "Feast of the Waters."

Dusk was falling when Mr. Martino announced that it was time to return to port. Just before lifting anchor, Mr. Gonzalez asked Alberto if he had seen the Phots. "No, it's been a while since I last saw them," he replied. "Let's look for them."

They found Chhak, Somsimen, and their parents standing together at the back of the boat, holding hands and smiling as they gazed at the waters of the Sacramento.

1. Why did Alberto want to plan a trip to a river with the Phot family?

____

____

____

2. Why did Chhak's eyes light up when he saw a picture of the Sacramento River?

____

____

3. How did Chhak and his family feel at the end of the story? How do you know?

____

____

____

____

____

____

4. What cultural details in the story help you understand the characters better?

____

____

____

____

____

____

The Pretty Pennies picket

Read the story. Then match each underlined word to its meaning listed below. Write the word next to its meaning.

"My jacket! It's too small for me now!" Ed said. "The shrinkage must have happened in the wash. I'm going to Sharp's store with my receipt to demand that they refund my money!"

His sister sighed. "Ed . . ."

"Mr. Sharp has always been courteous to me. I thought he was a sincere, honest businessman. I was wrong! What other revelations will I learn?"

"Ed, listen . . ."

"Don't try to talk me out of it, Sue. I won't be persuaded! Maybe I'll discover other injustices. I'll get my friends to form a picket line in front of Sharp's store. We'll protest his poor quality merchandise!"

"*Ed!* That's *my* jacket! I bought one just like yours but in a smaller size. I don't blame you for getting angry. It's human nature. But next time, don't jump to conclusions!"

	WORD	**MEANING**
1.	____________________	things that are bought or sold
2.	____________________	unfair acts
3.	____________________	the way most people behave in a certain situation
4.	____________________	talked into doing, thinking, or believing something
5.	____________________	the act or process of becoming smaller
6.	____________________	to give money back
7.	____________________	polite, considerate
8.	____________________	things that are made known for the first time
9.	____________________	honest

The Pretty Pennies picket

Look back at *The Pretty Pennies picket.* Then complete each sentence below.

1. Beth thought of making special uniforms for the Pretty Pennies to wear in the relay race against the Tiger Hunters because

2. The girls worked hard on designing and embroidering their T-shirts because

3. After they had washed their shirts, the Pretty Pennies became angry because

4. After the Pretty Pennies had spoken to Mr. Putterham about the shrunken uniforms, they became as mad as "wet hens" because

5. After talking to the sheriff, the Pretty Pennies felt "like a bunch of beaten soldiers" because

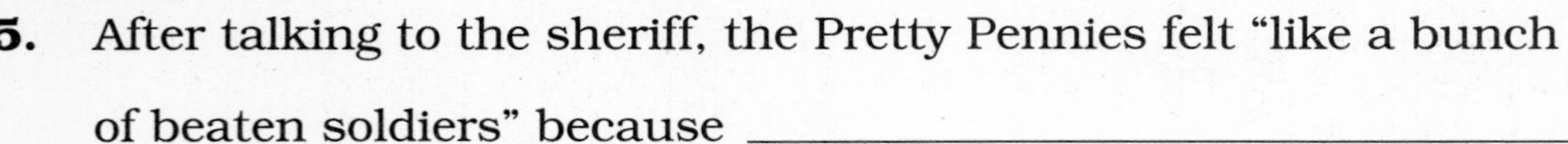

6. The Pretty Pennies and the Tiger Hunters set up a picket line in front of the Busy Bee Bargain Store because

7. At the end of the story, Beth said Mr. Putterham had finally done the right thing because

The Streets Are Free

In each group of words below, draw a line through the word that does not belong in the group. Then write why the other three words belong together. The first one has been done for you.

1. **release** ~~**arrest**~~ **free** **unchain**

All but *arrest* mean "to set free."

2. **poster** **sign** **banner** **speech**

3. **reserved** **available** **saved** **set aside**

4. **calming the waters** | **creating an uproar** | **disturbing the peace** | **causing a ruckus**

5. **intend** **plan** **aim** **wander**

Write about a time when you *intended* to do something, but it didn't work out as you planned.

Now write about a time when you witnessed a *ruckus.*

The Streets Are Free

Look back at the play *The Streets Are Free.* Then answer the questions below.

1. As the play opens, what is the main problem that Carlitos, Cheo, Camila, and the other children face? ______________________________

____

2. During their conversation with the librarian, what solution do the children come up with? ______________________________

____

3. Why do the children march to City Hall carrying banners and posters? ______________________________

____

4. What do the children do when the Mayor appears? ______________________________

____

5. What causes the Mayor to visit the empty lot? ______________________________

____

____

6. How do the children feel after the Mayor gives the speech and hangs the sign at the empty lot? ______________________________

____

____

7. How is the park finally built? ______________________________

____

Story Elements

As you read this story, think about the conflict between the characters and how this conflict is solved.

Best Friends

I hated my first day at Bay View School. Bay View had just opened because my old school, Jefferson, was too crowded. Starting a new school is never fun. But to make matters worse, by the end of that first day I was afraid I was losing my best friend.

Though half the students at Bay View had come from Jefferson, the other half were strangers. At Jefferson, everyone had known that Lindsey and I did everything together. At Bay View, no one treated us like best friends. Even Lindsey started acting as though we weren't.

The trouble began when we were assigned to study groups. I was assigned to Group B, and Lindsey was assigned to Group F. We had always been in the same group. But Lindsey didn't seem to mind. She just said, "This will be a nice change for you, Sarah."

We had to introduce ourselves to the other students in our groups and tell them about our interests. When I said I plan to be a veterinarian, a boy named Eddie said that his dad is a vet and that he likes animals, too. Dustin said he wants to be a pilot, and Adam said he likes to draw. They acted friendly, but I would rather have been with Lindsey.

She didn't seem to miss me. I could see her laughing with the kids in Group F.

Later that day things got worse. While Lindsey and I were eating lunch, she told me about a girl in her study group.

"Michelle is really nice. She told me about an after-school group that's going to put on plays," Lindsey said. "They asked me to paint the scenery!"

She always had been good at art. I hate acting and art. Why did she want to spend time with those people?

As Lindsey and I were leaving school, Eddie came up to me. "Hey, Sarah, do you want to walk home with me and see my dad's vet offices?"

"No. I always walk home with Lindsey."

As Eddie left, I looked to see if Lindsey had gotten the message about how best friends act.

She sighed unhappily. "Don't you want to make new friends here?"

"Why? We're best friends."

"I don't know if I can be best

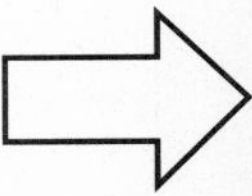

friends in the same way anymore." She suddenly ran off, leaving me to walk home alone.

I was almost crying by the time I got home. I found Dad in the yard.

"Dad, who's your best friend?" I asked.

Dad smiled. "Your mom."

I was puzzled. "Then why do you do so many things with other people?"

"For one thing, she and I don't enjoy all the same things," he said. "For another, we do enjoy sharing stories about the things we do with our other friends. Now, tell me what's on your mind."

I told him everything. That's when I realized that there was only one way to keep from losing Lindsey as my friend.

The next day, Lindsey hardly spoke to me and went off to sit with Michelle at lunchtime. I asked Eddie and Adam if they would like to join me for lunch. After they said they would, we walked over to Lindsey's table. I said "Hi," but Lindsey didn't look up.

I asked, "Is it okay if we join you, Lindsey? You know Eddie and Adam, don't you? Adam's an artist. He would like to paint scenery with you."

This time Lindsey did raise her head. She had a smile on her face. I grinned right back at her.

Answer these questions about *Best Friends*. Look back at the story if you need to.

1. Who are the two main characters of the story? ______________________

____

2. Describe the conflict in the story. ______________________

____

____

3. Write two of the events that make up the plot of the story.

Write the events in the order that they happen. ______________________

____

____

4. What is the resolution of the story? ______________________

____

The Doughnuts

Read each sentence. Choose a word or phrase from the box that means almost the same as the underlined words. Then write the word on the line.

labor saving devices	automatic
gadgets	improvements
up and coming	calamity
advanced	receipts

1. ______________ Hector works for a company that is headed for future success.

2. ______________ Kecia Krumble, the owner of the Krumble Cookie Company, has many new ideas that are ahead of the times.

3. ______________ She told Hector, "My cookie recipes and my modern machines are my secrets for success."

4. ______________ Each week changes that make something better are added to help the company become more successful.

5. ______________ One of these machines that are designed to reduce people's work is a cookie mixer that can mix twice as many cookies as the old one.

6. ______________ There is also a cookie cutter that is capable of operating by itself.

7. ______________ Other helpful mechanical objects flip the cookies when they have turned golden brown.

8. ______________ But today there has been one disaster after another. First, the cookie cutter stopped cutting, and the cookie flippers stopped flipping. Then the giant mixer stopped mixing. Finally, when Hector was struggling to fix the mixer, he slipped and fell head first into the huge tank of dough!

The Doughnuts

Look back at the story *The Doughnuts*. Think about what happens in the story. Then fill in the blanks to complete the story frame below.

One Friday night, Homer Price went to his Uncle Ulysses's lunch room to keep him company. When Homer arrived, Uncle Ulysses was busy oiling and cleaning the automatic doughnut machine. He asked Homer to finish putting the machine back together and ________________ ________________ while he went to the barber shop.

A "sandwich man" named ________________ came into the lunch room. Then a ________________________________ came into the lunch room. The rich lady helped Homer by ________________________. They loaded the doughnut machine with batter and pushed the "start" button.

The lady and her chauffeur left the lunch room. Homer pressed the "stop" button on the machine, but __________ ______________________________________. When Uncle Ulysses and the Sheriff arrived, ________________________ ____.

Then the rich lady returned to the lunch room because she ____________________________________. She offered a reward of one hundred dollars for the bracelet. Homer figured that the bracelet was probably in ________________ ________________. Then Homer offered the reward to anyone who ____.

The story ended happily when ________________________ ____.

To Space & Back

Use the words in the box to complete the passage that follows.

anchored	weightlessness	float
fluids	gravity	

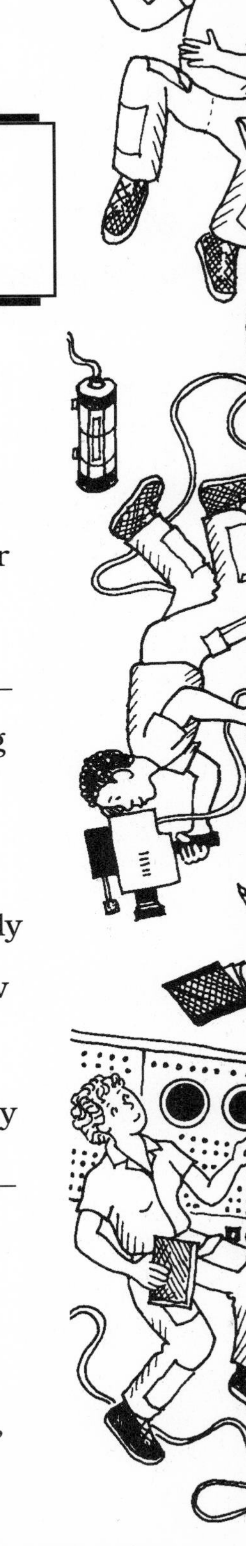

Living in a spacecraft that is traveling through space is very different than living on the surface of Earth. In space, the force of Earth's ________________ is too weak to pull astronauts and objects down. This makes the control center of a spaceship an unusual sight. Without gravity, books, pencils, tools, food, water, and even astronauts __________ through the air. Imagine being able to crawl across a ceiling or to hang in the middle of a room!

At first, many astronauts have trouble getting used to ________________. They paddle their arms and legs wildly and try to swim through the air. But they quickly learn how to get around the spacecraft with little effort.

Astronauts must also learn to store their tools when they are finished using them. Tools must be ________________ to the walls of the craft to keep them from floating away.

Drinking a glass of water is also different in space. Regular glasses can't be used for drinking because it is impossible to pour ________________ in space. To drink, astronauts must use a straw.

To Space & Back

If you need help with these words as you read the story, look in the glossary: anchored, gravity, weightless.

Before You Read Think about the questions you wrote on page 111 of your Journal. Try to answer these questions as you read the selection.

Read from page 291 through the last complete paragraph on page 295. Then come back to this page and answer questions 1 and 2.

1. What are some things the astronauts do before the launch? Use the launch countdown below to answer the question.

Launch minus four hours: ______________________________

____

____

Launch minus three hours: ______________________________

____

____

____

Launch minus one hour: ______________________________

____

____

2. What happens to the shuttle as the countdown continues?

Launch minus seven minutes: ______________________________

____

Launch minus 10 seconds: ______________________________

____

3 . . . 2 . . . 1 . . . : ______________________________

____

Read from the bottom of page 295 to the end of the first paragraph on page 300. Then answer question 3.

3. How does the shuttle's orbit compare to the flight of an airplane or a weather satellite? ______________________________

____

____

Read to the end of the selection. Then answer questions 4–7.

4. How is being in space different from being on Earth? ______________________________

____

____

____

5. How is being in space the same as being on Earth? ______________________________

____

____

____

6. How do astronauts eat in space? ______________________________

____

____

____

____

7. How do astronauts sleep in space? ______________________________

____

____

After You Read Look back over your answers. If you had trouble understanding anything, reread the part that you did not understand.

To Space & Back

Look over *To Space & Back.*
Then answer each question below.

1. What are some of the things the astronauts have to do from the time they wake up until blast-off? ______

2. How does Sally Ride describe the first eight and one-half minutes of her journey into space? ______

3. How does weightlessness affect the astronauts' movements? ______

4. How does weightlessness affect the way food is prepared and eaten? ______

5. How do the astronauts manage to sleep while in orbit? ______

Mars

Use the words in the box to complete the following sentences.

craters	astronomer	canals
planet	volcanoes	meteorites
atmosphere		

1. During the discussion in science class, Danny looked puzzled. "A large body that moves around the sun is a __________________, correct?" he asked.
2. "Yes," answered Mrs. Cawley. "Now who can tell me whether the surface of Earth's moon has any wide, hollowed-out areas, or __________________?"
3. Carmen answered, "Yes, it does. The craters might have been caused by __________________ that fell from outer space."
4. Then Kwong spoke up. "When I grow up, I would like to be an __________________ and study the planets, moons, and stars."
5. Mrs. Cawley said, "An astronomer once thought he saw lines that looked like waterways, or __________________, on the surface of a planet. But it was later discovered that these lines are actually deep channels that look like dry riverbeds."
6. Mrs. Cawley added, "Many planets have mountains called __________________ that sometimes erupt and spill lava."
7. "Now, class, your assignment is to write about why the gases that make up Earth's __________________ are important to us."

Mars

Look back at *Mars*. Then write two or more details from the article that support each statement below. The first one has been completed for you.

1. Mars takes longer than Earth to orbit the sun. **Mars is 50 million miles farther away from the sun than Earth is, so its path is longer. Mars takes about 687 Earth days to orbit the sun once.**

2. At one time, many people thought there might be life on Mars.

3. Mars appears to be a dusty planet.

4. The United States landed two spacecraft on Mars.

5. The surface of Mars is dangerous to unprotected humans.

6. Today, most scientists do not believe that life as we know it exists on Mars.

Main Ideas, Supporting Details, and Fact and Opinion

Read the article below. Then answer the questions that follow the article.

Mount St. Helens Blows Its Top

1. In January of 1980, Mount St. Helens, a mountain peak in Washington State, looked the same as it had for hundreds of winters. The mountain, which was surrounded by frozen lakes and dense forests, was covered with a thick blanket of snow. From a distance, the mountain looked peaceful and serene.
2. In March of that year the once-peaceful mountain began to change. Two earthquakes shook the ground around the mountain. Then the mountain began to shoot huge clouds of steam and ash into the air.
3. These changes did not surprise scientists. They had known for a long time that the mountain was a volcano. Mount St. Helens is part of the Cascade mountain range. Most of the Cascade mountains are volcanoes. Mount St. Helens also had a history of volcanic eruptions and had been active as recently as 1857.
4. Then in April of 1980 something happened that alarmed scientists. They discovered a dangerous, rapidly growing bulge in the side of the mountain. They warned that this bulge, which was expanding by five feet a day, might set off an avalanche or an eruption. But scientists could not predict the violence of the eruption that was soon to follow.
5. On May 18, 1980, Mount St. Helens exploded with such force that it nearly blew itself to bits. Rocks, some as large as trucks, shot up twelve miles into the air, hurled by the powerful blasts that shook the mountain. An avalanche of falling rocks roared down the mountainside, shattering trees like matchsticks. The avalanche was followed by rivers of mud. Thousands of forest animals and more than fifty people were killed. The volcanic explosion was so powerful, it blasted away a thousand feet from the height of the peak. Mount St. Helens was once

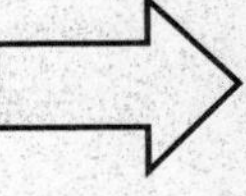

Washington's most beautiful mountain peak. After the eruption, all that was left of the mountain was a large, smoking crater.

6. Wind carried ash from the explosion for hundreds of miles. In the city of Yakima, Washington, eighty-five miles northeast of Mount St. Helens, the ash made the noon sky as dark as night. People had to wear masks to keep from choking on the ash-clogged air.

7. Mount St. Helens erupted again several times after the first explosion in 1980. Altogether, the eruptions of Mount St. Helens caused more than $1.5 billion worth of damage to property, crops, and forests. Most living things within a fifteen-mile range of the exploding mountaintop were destroyed. Ash from the eruptions clogged streets and machinery in Washington, Oregon, and parts of Idaho and Montana for months afterward. The eruptions of Mount St. Helens showed just how surprising — and powerful — nature can be.

1. What is the topic of this article? ____________________

2. What is the main idea of the second paragraph of the article?

____

3. Write two details from the second paragraph that support the main idea.

A. ____________________

B. ____________________

4. Write the main idea and three supporting details from the seventh paragraph.

Main Idea: ____________________

Supporting Details:

A. ____________________

B. ____________________

C. ____________________

5. Write the sentence in the fifth paragraph that expresses an opinion.

____

Humans on Mars?

Imagine that you are a scientist who is being interviewed by a reporter. Write your answer to each of the reporter's questions. In each answer, use the word from the box that means the same as the underlined word or words in the question. The first question has been done for you.

launch	environment	scan	resources
base	energy	voyage	

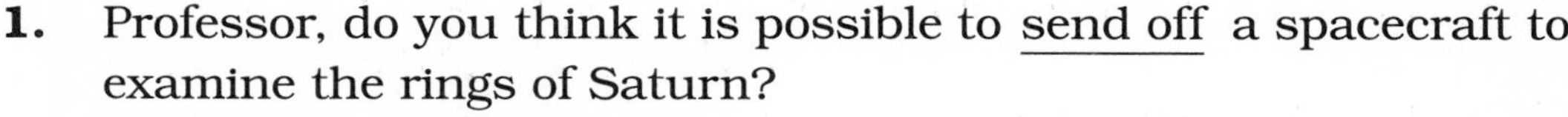

1. Professor, do you think it is possible to send off a spacecraft to examine the rings of Saturn?

   We hope to *launch* a rocket to Saturn within ten years.

2. What will we need to do to prepare for such a long journey ?

3. What kind of supplies will we need to build the spacecraft?

4. Will we need to build an emergency headquarters on the moon?

5. What source of power would such a headquarters use?

6. How will the astronauts examine Saturn's rings?

7. How will they study the surrounding conditions on Saturn?

Humans on Mars?

Before You Read Recall the questions you wrote on page 121 of your Journal. Try to find the answers to these questions as you read the selection.

Read page 337. Then come back to this page and answer the question below.

Which three places might NASA explore in the future?

____

____

____

Read pages 338–339. Then fill in the part of the chart that tells about a moon base.

Moon Base	Reasons to Build a Moon Base	Steps That Need to Be Taken
	____________	____________
	____________	____________
	____________	____________
	____________	____________
	____________	____________
	____________	____________
	____________	____________
	____________	____________
	____________	____________
	____________	____________
	____________	____________
	____________	____________

Read from page 340 to the end of the selection. Then complete the rest of the chart on page 45.

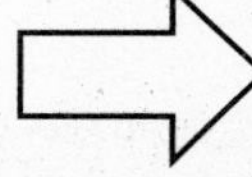

On to Mars

Reasons to Explore Mars

Steps That Need to Be Taken

Mission to Planet Earth

Reasons to Explore Earth from Space

Steps That Need to Be Taken

After You Read Review what you have written on these pages. Then answer these questions:

What big decision does the U.S. space program face? ______

What will be required, no matter which plan is chosen? ______

Humans on Mars?

Look back at *Humans on Mars?* Complete each sentence below by writing details from the article.

1. NASA is considering exploration of the moon because it ______________________

2. A NASA moon base might be used for a place to ______________________

3. NASA will probably send robot probes to Mars before people because ______________________

4. A space station orbiting Earth might be useful for space exploration because ______________________

5. Some experts believe that Earth and its features should be explored from space next so that scientists can ______________________

6. Before any of these plans go into action, scientists need to ______________________

The Weaving of a Dream

Read the story below. Then use the underlined words to complete the sentences that follow.

Once there was a poor orphan named Hans who wandered the countryside begging for food. One day, Hans became lost during a blizzard. A widow found him lying in the snow. When she saw that he was breathing, she knew that he was not dead but only unconscious. The widow decided that if she didn't help the boy, she would feel remorse later. So she carried him to her warm home.

When Hans awoke, he told the widow about the hardships he had been forced to endure. She was filled with such grief she cried. She then handed Hans a thick piece of brocade and told him she was going to teach him to weave fabric.

Hans learned quickly to use a shuttle to pull the thread through her loom. Soon he was able to weave faster than the widow herself. Together, they made fabrics with many tiny details woven into them. The pictures of birds and flowers woven into each brocade were so lifelike that they looked real. People from miles around bought the beautiful brocades, and Hans never had to beg for food again.

1. To ____________ is to pass threads over and under one another.
2. It is often very difficult to ____________ hardship.
3. The word ____________ means "deep sorrow."
4. Someone who is ____________ cannot think or feel.
5. Some weavings show pictures that look real, or ____________.
6. The tool used in weaving to pull the thread is the ____________.
7. A large picture is made up of many small ____________.
8. A ____________ is a thick cloth that has raised designs.

The Weaving of a Dream

Look back at *The Weaving of a Dream.* Choose the word or words that best complete each statement below and write them in the blank space. Then, on the lines that follow each statement, write the reason for your choice.

1. When the brocade vanished in the wind, the old widow was ________________.

   short-tempered   heartbroken   anxious

   ____

   ____

2. After hearing what had to be done to recover the brocade, both Leme and Letuie felt ________________.

   courageous   frightened   curious

   ____

   ____

3. When Leje heard what he had to do to recover the brocade, he felt ________________.

   determined   terrified   nervous

   ____

   ____

4. When the red fairy saw that her copy of the brocade couldn't compare to the old woman's brocade, she ________________.

   set fire to the brocade   began work on another brocade   wove herself into the brocade

   ____

   ____

5. After Leje returned with the brocade and the details from the brocade became real, Leje and his mother were ________________.

   overjoyed   anxious   depressed

   ____

   ____

The Orphan Boy

Read the newspaper article below. Choose a word from the box that has almost the same meaning as the underlined word or words after each number. Then write the word on the numbered line below the article.

curiosity	prospered	majesty	fortune
recognition	barren	compounds	deeds

Drought Continues on Great Plains

No rain is in sight for most of the Great Plains today. This drought-stricken region has had very little rain for the last four months. Crops are parched and grazing land for cattle looks (1) empty of living things.

Because of the drought, wheat farmers, who only last year (2) did well, are now wondering if they will be able to harvest any wheat at all. Ranchers, who had good (3) luck with plenty of rain last year, are now searching for new grazing land. Many ranchers have moved their cattle to (4) fenced-in areas and are giving their cattle feed.

In (5) awareness of the drought, many government agents have traveled to the Great Plains. Farmers say that these agents have come only out of (6) a desire to know. These farmers don't trust the agents' words. They are waiting to judge the government's (7) actions.

After four dry months, the entire countryside looks dusty and withered. Until the drought ends the (8) glory and splendor of the Great Plains will be only a memory.

1. ____________________
2. ____________________
3. ____________________
4. ____________________
5. ____________________
6. ____________________
7. ____________________
8. ____________________

The Orphan Boy

Think about *The Orphan Boy*. Read the statements below. Then complete the sentences that follow by writing details from the story that support each statement.

1. Kileken the orphan boy had an amazing ability for doing chores. Before the old man woke on the first day, Kileken

___

Before the sunrise of the second day, Kileken ___

___

2. During the drought, Kileken seemed to have magical powers.

Despite the drought, the cattle ___

During the drought, more calves ___

3. Kileken refused to tell the old man how he managed to feed the cattle during the drought.

Kileken told the old man ___

___

Kileken explained that the old man's fortune would end if ___

___

4. The old man's shadow tempted him to satisfy his curiosity.

The shadow told the old man ___

___

The shadow convinced the old man to ___

___

5. The old man learned Kileken's secret, but at a price.

When Kileken found out that the old man had followed him and discovered his secret, Kileken ___

___

After Kileken disappeared, ___

___

Cause-Effect/Theme and Symbolism

Read the folktale that follows. Think about what happens and why it happens. Then follow the directions after the story.

The Three Nephews

Once upon a time there was a wise king who had no children. He did, however, have three nephews. One day he sent for Gustav, Rudolf, and Leon to come to his mountaintop castle.

He told them, "Here are five gold pieces for each of you. Go down into my kingdom and do your best to be successful. Then come back in two years and I will decide which of you is most fit to rule my kingdom when I die."

Gustav spent his gold in merrymaking with all the rich dukes and duchesses of the kingdom until they were tired of him. Finally, Gustav ran out of his gold and the only job he could find was counting the toothpicks in a castle pantry.

Rudolf took his five gold coins to a jewelry maker and had him make five brass rings covered with gold. Rudolf went to the next town and sold the rings, saying they were pure gold. Then he used the money to make ten more gold-covered brass rings. This was how he lived, slipping from town to town before his trick was discovered. At the end of two years, he had one hundred gold pieces.

With his gold, Leon bought a peddler's pack filled with all sorts of things people needed. Then he hiked through the countryside selling needles, thimbles, ribbons, bows, pots, spoons, and little tin whistles. Soon he had saved enough money to buy a cart and a donkey to pull it. At the end of two years, he had saved enough money to buy a large shop.

When the two years were up, all three men started back to the mountaintop castle. As Gustav climbed the mountain, the air grew colder and he shivered. Halfway up, he saw a red and yellow wagon with three cloaks hanging on it. One was of plain wool, one of velvet, and one of silk.

"I'll borrow a cloak," he thought. "It will keep me warm and make a fine show before the king." So he took the velvet cloak and went on his way.

Not long after, Rudolf came to the wagon. "Anyone with two cloaks has one to spare," he thought. "Besides, a fine cloak will make a good show before the king." So he took the silk cloak.

Finally Leon, shivering, came to the wagon. He knocked on the door, which was opened just a crack by a shadowy figure. "I will give you a gold piece for that wool cloak of yours," Leon said. A hand reached out and took Leon's gold, and Leon went on his way.

When all three nephews stood before the king, Gustav boasted to his uncle, "By my beautiful velvet cloak you can see that I have an important job with a great duke."

"By these gold rings and the silk cloak I wear, Uncle, you can tell that I am a great gold merchant," boasted Rudolf.

"I have a good, busy shop in a market town," said Leon proudly.

The other two nephews laughed, but the king silenced them. "Perhaps someday you two will also learn the value of honest work," he said. Then he pointed out the window to the meadow, where the nephews were surprised to see the red and yellow wagon. "I am the owner of that wagon and also of the cloaks," the king said.

And at that, he handed Leon a gold coin. "I am an honest man myself, Leon. I am making you a gift of the cloak. My kingdom will someday be yours as well."

1. Think about the decisions the three nephews make after the king gives them the gold. Then, on the lines below, write why you think the nephews behave as they do.

Gustav ______________________________

____

Rudolf ______________________________

____

Leon ______________________________

____

2. What do you think is the theme, or message, of this tale?

____

____

3. The three cloaks are important objects in the story. If the fancy cloaks that Gustav and Rudolf chose to wear can be seen as symbols of the two men's laziness and dishonesty, what might the wool cloak symbolize?

____

Her Seven Brothers

Write each word from the box below next to its meaning.

embroider	porcupine quills	immensity
designs	courting	storyteller
patterns	powers	spirits

Words	***Meanings***
________	the sharp, stiff, thin spines on a porcupine's body
________	arrangements of parts and colors on something such as cloth or paper
________	to decorate by sewing designs with a needle and thread
________	the ways that lines and shapes are arranged to form designs
________	someone who tells stories
________	ghosts
________	to try to win the love of a person one wishes to marry
________	great size
________	a person or group of people who have great control over others

On the lines below, write about an interesting design you have seen. ________________________________

____

____

____

Her Seven Brothers

Look back at the story *Her Seven Brothers*. Complete the story frame below with details from the story.

Long ago there was a girl who could speak to the animals and who could understand the spirits of all things. The girl had a vision of seven lonely brothers. The young girl planned to find the brothers and ask them if ______________________

____.

When the girl found the brothers, the youngest brother was not surprised to see her because he ________________

____.

The girl gave the brothers ______________________

____.

The girl and her seven new brothers lived happily together until one day when the buffalo chief sent a calf demanding that ______________________________________

____.

After the little boy refused to part with the sister, the buffalo chief sent a ________________ and then an ____________ to bring the girl back to him. Each time the boy said ______

____.

Suddenly the girl and her brothers heard ____________

____.

The youngest boy was able to save his sister and brothers. He made a pine tree appear by ____________________.

The girl and her brothers climbed the tree and jumped into the sky. They became ________________________.

The Blossoms Meet the Vulture Lady

Read the story and think about the meaning of each underlined word. Then write the word next to its meaning below.

The raccoons had raided Hattie's garbage can again last night, and her misery showed on her face. She felt so frustrated. Hattie hated any cruelty, and she would never hurt the raccoons, but this was annoying! "If I were an inventor, I'd make a raccoon-proof garbage can. I'd earn a fortune with that invention!" she muttered to herself. Then she had an inspiration. She'd build a cage to trap the raccoons and then set them free in the State Forest!

Hattie wanted the cage to be safe and sturdy, so she spent a long time on its construction. Even Hattie, who was a perfectionist, was happy with the final results.

Unfortunately, the raccoons just ignored it! But she did catch a cat. "That's it," she groaned in despair. "I give up!"

WORDS	MEANINGS
1. ________	the act or process of building
2. ________	a good idea that comes suddenly
3. ________	not being able to do what could or should be done
4. ________	mean, harsh, or painful treatment
5. ________	someone who wants things to be perfect
6. ________	a strong feeling of unhappiness
7. ________	the feeling of losing hope; giving up
8. ________	a person who makes something new and original
9. ________	something invented or made for the first time

The Blossoms Meet the Vulture Lady

Look back at *The Blossoms Meet the Vulture Lady.* Use story details to complete the missing parts of the chart.

Characters' Problems	***What Characters Did***
1. Junior was missing from the Blossoms' dinner table.	1. ______________________________
2. The trap door had clicked shut, so ______________________________	2. Junior tried to get out by working the wire mesh and latches loose with his fingers.
3. Junior knew that if he grabbed and held Mud, Mud would howl. But Mud ______________________________	3. Junior lured Mud to the cage with balls of hamburger meat until he could grab the dog's bandanna.
4. The Blossom family had to find Junior before it got dark and before the storm hit.	4. They followed ______________________________
5. Mad Mary thought that ______________________________	5. Mad Mary opened the door of the cage and "rescued" the sleeping boy. Then she carried him to the safety of her cave.
6. The Blossoms finally found the coyote cage, but ______________________________	

The Gift-Giver

Match the words in the box with the definitions below. Write each word on the line in front of its definition. On the lines that follow each definition, write a sentence that uses the word.

foster home	authorities	embarrass
rumors	acquaintances	stoop

1. ____________ People whom you know, but who are not as well known to you as are your friends: ____________

____

____

2. ____________ To make someone nervous or uncomfortable:

____

____

3. ____________ Unchecked information that is spread by word of mouth: ____________

____

4. ____________ A platform or flight of stairs leading to the door of a house or apartment building: ____________

____

5. ____________ People who have controlling power: ____________

____

____

6. ____________ A place where orphans and homeless children can live: ____________

____

The Gift-Giver

Look back at *The Gift-Giver*. Think about the major events of the story. Then complete the sentences below to describe what happened.

1. At the beginning of the story, Big Russell is mad because ______________________

____

____

2. Amir tries to calm Big Russell by ______________________

____

____

3. When Yellow Bird enters the gym, Doris laughs because ______________________

____

____

4. Even without Sherman, the fifth-grade basketball team ______________________

____

5. The morning after the basketball game Doris becomes angry with Mickey and Dotty because ______________________

____

____

6. Some of the fifth graders see Sherman and try to talk to him, but ______________________

____

7. When Doris finds Sherman in the basement, he tells her ______________________

____

____

8. Doris and Amir try to help Sherman by ______________________

____

____

Cause-Effect Relationships and Visualizing

As you read the story below, try to form a mental picture of the characters and the events. Also think about the story's cause-effect relationships. Then follow the directions on page 60.

Welcome to Lone Tree

"Here you go," said the cheerful driver as he swung their battered suitcase down off the bus. "This is Lone Tree. I don't see your aunty anywhere, but don't worry. She'll be around 'cause she's real dependable."

Eliza grabbed her five-year-old brother's crutches and helped him down the steps. Eliza and Scotty stepped off the bus and looked around in disbelief. They were standing on the cracked pavement of a long-closed gas station. Only a shack, a faded sign, and a gas pump remained, standing guard like long-forgotten soldiers.

The bus doors squeaked shut, and the silver-blue bus roared down the highway, belching fumes.

Eliza watched it disappear as a cold, empty feeling grew inside her. "We're in the middle of nowhere," she thought. She stared at the thin line of highway and the telephone poles following it out of sight. There was little else to see except a few prickly bushes set into a dusty-brown desert. "So much for the great scenery out West," she sighed. "Some vacation this is!" She brushed a brown curl away from her thin face.

"I'm hot and I'm hungry," murmured her brother. His nap had left his soft black hair sticking out this way and that.

Eliza pulled the bright red jacket off his body and tied it around his waist. "I'm sure Aunt Millie will have something for us to eat. Let's go find her," she suggested, trying to sound cheerful.

Scotty slipped his backpack onto his shoulders. Eliza picked up the suitcase, and they began walking.

Soon, they found themselves on a short street with some old, tired buildings on either side. The pavement on the street was cracked and bumpy. Sand had drifted everywhere, settling in patches on the pavement. The whole town seemed hot and dry, like Eliza's face and throat. "Where is everyone?" asked Scotty, his round eyes growing even larger.

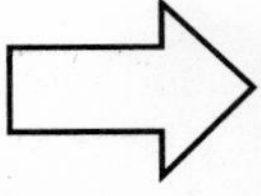

Just then the two children heard a clatter of hooves. From a side street next to a hotel a woman appeared, riding a chestnut mare and leading a second horse behind her.

"You're earlier than I expected!" the rider hollered to the children as she rode over to them. Then she jumped down and grinned. "Come here and say 'howdy' to your Aunt Millie. My how you've grown!" She scooped each child up in a quick bear hug. "I saddled up old Patsy here," she continued, patting the second horse. "I figured you might like to ride back to the ranch western-style!"

Scotty's eyes grew large again. Then they lit up. And, after breathing a sigh of relief, Eliza smiled too.

1. Choose one character from the story and describe your mental picture of that character. Use details from the story and others that you added. ______________________________

____

____

____

____

2. Choose one story event and describe your mental picture of what happened. ______________________________

____

____

____

____

____

3. Think about how Scotty and Eliza feel at the end of the story. How have their feelings changed since they got off the bus? What causes their feelings to change? ______________________________

____

____

____

The Mouse and the Motorcycle

Use the words in the box to replace the underlined words in the sentences below.

exhaust pipes	predicament	incinerator	reckless
coast	threshold	momentum	

1. The mouse jumped onto the toy motorcycle, put his paw on the hand clutch, and roared off. Puffs of smoke came from the pipes that carry off waste gases. ________________
2. The shiny chromium mufflers, metal fenders, and wire spokes gleamed in the moonlight. As the motorcycle built up speed it went faster and faster. ________________
3. As soon as the mouse came to the top of a hill, he let up on the gas so that he could glide without power down the hill.

   ____
4. Suddenly, he found himself in a very unfortunate situation. A big trash can was in the way, and he skidded into it.

   ____
5. Luckily, he hit the trash can and not the furnace for burning trash. ________________
6. The mouse brushed himself off and made a vow — he would not be so careless again. ________________
7. Soon the mouse would be on his way. He was at the beginning of a great adventure! ________________

The Mouse and the Motorcycle

Before You Read Turn to Journal page 177 and think about the strategy you have chosen to read this selection. Keep your strategy in mind as you read.

Read pages 480–484. Then come back to this page and answer these three questions.

Why do the Gridleys stay at the Mountain View Inn? ____________________

____

____

Who might be the one who is watching the Gridleys as they arrive in their hotel rooms? ____________________

____

How do Keith and his mother each feel about mice? ____________________

____

____

Read pages 485–494. Then answer the four questions that follow.

Why does the boy's toy motorcycle cause Ralph to feel eager, excited, curious, and impatient all at once? ____________________

____

Why does Ralph's mother worry about him? ____________________

____

____

What happens to spoil Ralph's first motorcycle ride? ____________________

____

____

____

Because of Ralph's accident with the motorcycle, what dangers does he face? ____

____

____

Read to the end of the selection. Then answer the questions that follow.

How do Keith and Ralph meet? ______________________________

____

____

____

What is the secret behind starting the motorcycle engine? __________

____

____

How does Ralph feel about riding the toy motorcycle? ______________

____

____

Why does Keith enjoy watching Ralph ride the motorcycle? __________

____

____

____

After You Read Think about the things Ralph does and says in the story. How would you describe him? What leads you to think as you do?

____

____

____

The Mouse and the Motorcycle

Look back at *The Mouse and the Motorcycle.* Choose a word from the box that best describes how the character felt in each sentence below. Write it on the line. Then explain the reason for your answer. The first one has been done for you.

excited	surprised	happy
terrified	envious	sad

1. Keith had Room 215 all to himself. **Happy; he could play with his cars and explore without getting into trouble. He said he liked the idea.**

2. Ralph first saw the toy motorcycle. ______

3. The telephone rang right next to Ralph. ______

4. Ralph found himself inside the wastebasket. ______

5. Keith discovered Ralph inside the wastebasket. ______

6. Keith watched the mouse ride his toy motorcycle. ______

Parts of a Book

Some of the parts of a book are listed in the box. Read the questions that follow. Then write the name of the part of a book that you would use to find the answer to each question.

title page	glossary	table of contents
index	copyright page	

1. Who wrote *Passport to Australia*? ____________________
2. What does the word *refract* mean? ____________________
3. When was the book *Tropical Rain Forests* published?

   ____
4. Is the topic *explorers* discussed in an American history book?

   ____
5. Who published *The Stonewalkers* by Vivien Alcock?

   ____
6. On which page does Chapter 4 start in the book *Our Independence and the Constitution*? ____________________
7. On which page does a health book explain how your hearing works? ____________________

Look for the following information in your Anthology. Write the information on the lines.

Book title: ____________________

The year the book was published: ____________________

The first word in the glossary: ____________________

The page number where the story *Where's Buddy?* begins: ____________________

Using an Index

Use this index from a book about life on the Western Frontier to answer the questions. Write the answers on the line.

1. In what order are the main topics listed in the index? ____________
2. What subtopics are listed under *Mining*? ____________

____
3. Which subtopic under *Mining* might tell you about the tools miners used? ____________
4. Under which topic would you find more information about trading posts? ____________
5. On which pages would you find information about the daily lives of farmers on the Western Frontier? ____________
6. On which page would you find a picture of a stagecoach? ____________
7. How many pages have information about law and order in the Old West? ____________
8. On which pages might you find information about covered wagon trails? ____________

Following Directions

Read these directions, and study the pictures. Then complete the sentences below.

Make a Piñata!

Follow these directions to make the "hit" of the party — a colorful piñata.

First, collect everything you will need: an old beach ball, petroleum jelly, old newspapers, wheat or wallpaper paste, masking tape, treats, three feet or more of sturdy string, poster paints, and paintbrushes. Then cut or tear the newspaper into two-inch by four-inch strips, and prepare the paste.

Next, blow up the ball, and coat it with petroleum jelly to keep the paper strips from sticking to the ball. Dip strips of newspaper into the paste, and apply them to the ball, one strip at a time. Cover the entire ball except for a small area around the mouthpiece. Continue until you've added about ten layers of strips. Let the piñata dry for about ten days.

When it is dry, let the air out of the ball, and pull the ball out of the hole you left around the mouthpiece. Next, poke two holes into the top of the piñata, and attach the string. Then put small toys and other treats inside through the opening you left for the mouthpiece. Cover the opening with masking tape.

Finally, paint the piñata with bright, colorful designs, and allow it to dry. Gather your friends together, and watch the fun begin as blindfolded players try to hit the piñata and break it open to get to the treats inside!

1. The first thing to do after you read the directions is to ________

____

2. Just before you paste the strips onto the beach ball, you should

____

3. Let the air out of the beach ball after ________

4. Cover the opening left by the beach ball after ________

____

5. The last step to finish the piñata is to ________

Card Catalog

Decide in which card catalog drawer you would look to find information about each item described below. Beside each item, write the letter or letters of the drawer in which you would look. Then write whether the card would be an author, title, or subject card. The first one is done for you.

	Drawer	Type of Card
1. The book *Escalante*	Di–E	title
2. The book *The Cricket in Times Square*		
3. Facts on the Industrial Revolution		
4. A book about magic tricks		
5. Books by Laura Ingalls Wilder		
6. The book *A Handful of Stars*		
7. A book about Cambodia		
8. Books by Mary Rodgers		
9. Information on nuclear energy		
10. The book *An Enemy at Green Knowe*		
11. The history of Japan		
12. The book *Sojourner Truth*		
13. Books by Sid Fleischman		

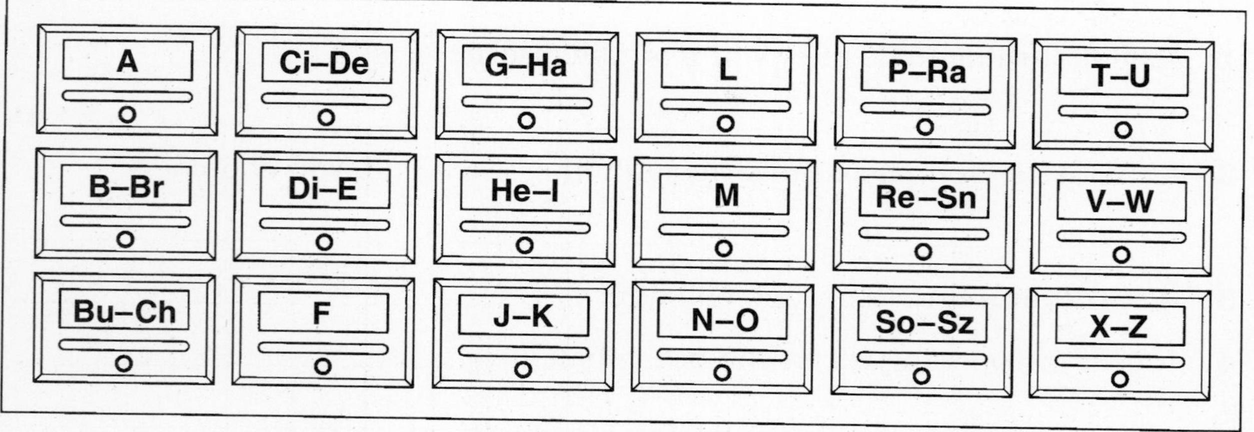

Look at these cards from the card catalog. Then use the information from them to answer the questions.

Subject card

	ENDANGERED SPECIES
639	Rinard, Judith
R	Wildlife: making a comeback
	National Geographic Society,
	1987

1. What is the title of the book? ____________________
2. Who wrote it? ____________________
3. What is the call number of the book? ____________________

Title card

599.74	Project panda watch
S	by Miriam Schlein. Illustrated
	by Robert Shetterly.
	Atheneum, 1984

4. What is the title of the book? ____________________
5. When was it published? ____________________
6. Who illustrated it? ____________________

Author card

591.5	Banks, Martin
B	Endangered wildlife. Vero
	Beach, FL: Rourke
	Enterprises, 1987

7. What is the title of the book? ____________________
8. Who wrote it? ____________________
9. Who published the book? ____________________

Using the Library

Decide whether each card lists a fiction or a nonfiction book. Write *Fiction* or *Nonfiction* on the first line. Then refer to the library diagram below to find the shelf on which you would look for that book. Write the number of the shelf on the second line. The first card is done for you.

	Nonfiction				Fiction			
Shelf	**1**	**2**	**3**	**4**	**5**	**6**	**7**	**8**
Number	000-399	400-599	600-799	800-999	A-F	G-L	M-R	S-Z

1.

612 E — The human body: the heart
Elgin, Kathleen

Nonfiction Shelf Number **3**

2.

398.2 S — Sleator, William
The angry moon

__________ Shelf Number ____

3.

568 A — Dinosaur mountain: graveyard of the past
Arnold, Caroline

__________ Shelf Number ____

4.

The borrowers
Norton, Mary

__________ Shelf Number ____

5.

919.4 B — Blunden, Godfrey
The land and people of Australia

__________ Shelf Number ____

6.

Cleaver, Vera
The mock revolt

__________ Shelf Number ____

The next time you go to the library, use what you have learned to find a book by an author, or a book about a topic, of your choosing.

Using an Encyclopedia

Read each question below. Write the key word you would look up in an encyclopedia to find the answer. Then write the encyclopedia volume number that would contain the information. The first question has been done for you.

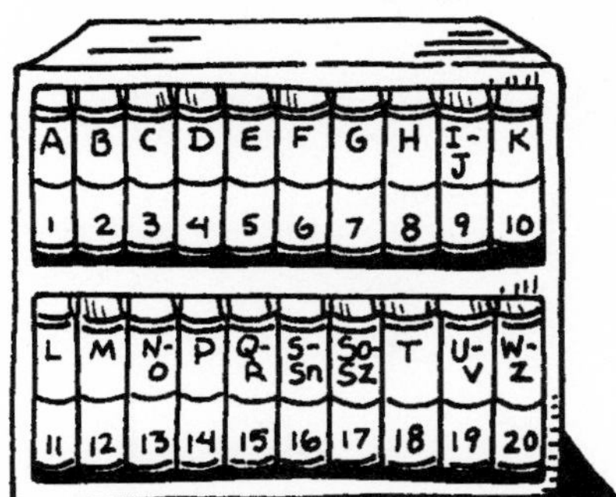

	Question	Key Word	Volume
1.	Through what countries does the Nile River flow?	**Nile**	**13**
2.	In what countries might the jackal be found?	__________	_____
3.	Why are opals considered to be such unusual gemstones?	__________	_____
4.	How high is the highest waterfall?	__________	_____

Look at these section headings from an encyclopedia article about oceans. Decide which section might have information that answers each question below. Write the heading on the line.

OCEANS

Currents, Tides, and Moving Water
Seawater's Chemical Makeup
Living Things in the Oceans
Studying the Oceans

5. What new discoveries have scientists made about water deep in the Red Sea? ____________________

6. What are the oceans' smallest plants and animals called? ____________________

7. Why are there waves in the oceans? ____________________

Reading Maps

Use this political map of Maine, New Hampshire, and Vermont to answer the questions below.

1. What country shares a national border with all three states?

    ____

2. What large body of water makes up most of the southeastern border of Maine? ___________________

3. With what state does Vermont share its eastern border?

    ____

4. What river flows along New Hampshire's western border?

    ____

5. What river flows through the central part of Maine? ___________________

    This river flows through what city? ___________________

6. What is the capital of Maine? ___________________

7. Which city lies closest to Lake Champlain? ___________________

8. If you were traveling from Augusta, Maine, to Burlington, Vermont, in what general direction would you be traveling?

    ____

9. What is the approximate number of miles between Concord, New Hampshire, and Augusta, Maine? ___________________

Reading Diagrams

Read the paragraphs and study the diagram. Then write the answer to each question.

The Glider

The glider is an airplane without an engine. To get a glider into the air, a car or truck pulls it with a rope. When the glider is going fast enough, it soars into the air, and the pilot releases the towrope.

In the air, the pilot steers the glider by moving a stick that raises and lowers the ailerons, making the glider roll right or left when turning. The stick also controls the elevator, which makes the nose of the glider go up or down. The rudder is controlled by foot pedals. It moves the glider's nose to the right or left to keep the plane flying smoothly.

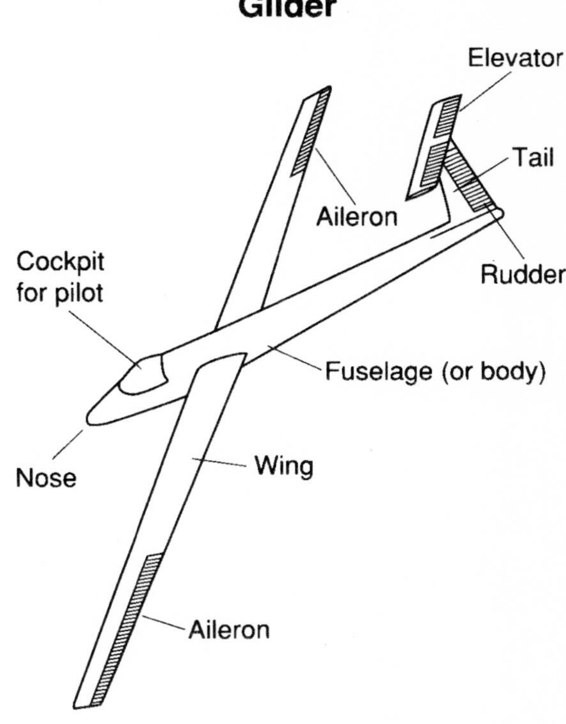

1. Where does the glider pilot sit? ______________________________

2. How does the pilot steer the glider? ______________________________

____

3. What parts of the glider does the stick control? ______________________________

____

4. Where are the ailerons located? ______________________________

5. Where is the elevator? ______________________________

6. What does the rudder do? ______________________________

____

7. Where is the rudder located? ______________________________

Graphs — Circle and Line

Study the circle graph and the line graph. Then read the questions below. Write your answers on the lines.

Number of Students Volunteering for Special Projects, from January Through June 1993

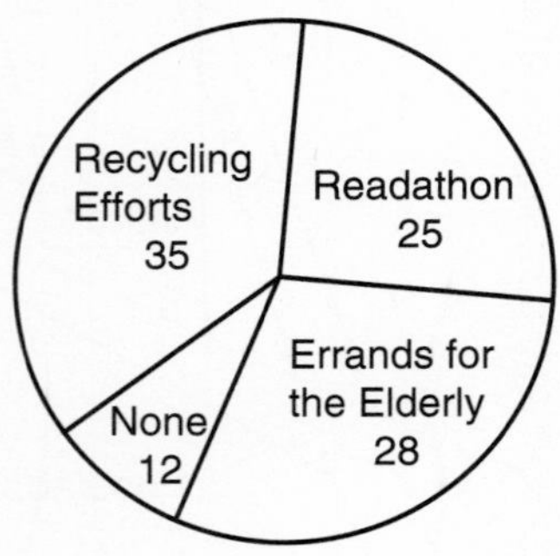

Average Amount of Time Each Student Spent on Special Projects, from January Through June 1993

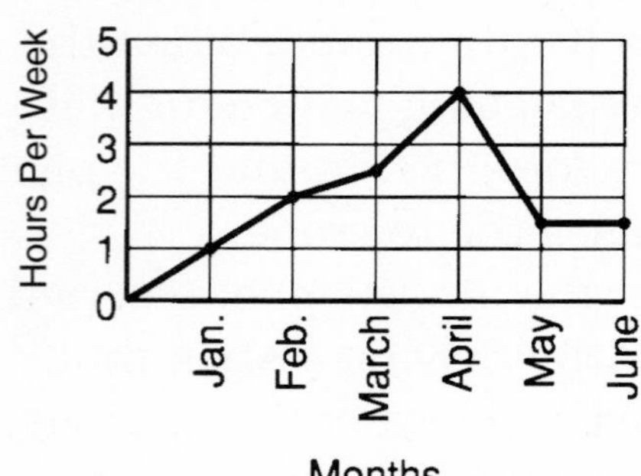

1. What does the circle graph show? ______________________

____

____

____

2. What do the labels and numbers on this circle graph tell you?

____

____

____

____

____

3. How many students participated in Errands for the Elderly?

____

4. Which project had the most student participation?

____

5. What does the line graph show?

____

____

____

____

____

6. About how many hours per week did each student spend on special projects in February?

__________ In April? __________

7. During which two months was student participation about the same? ______________________

8. During which month did students spend the most time participating in special projects?

____

Reading Tables

This table gives the daily schedule of rides at a space-age fantasy park called Space City. Use information from the table to answer the questions below it.

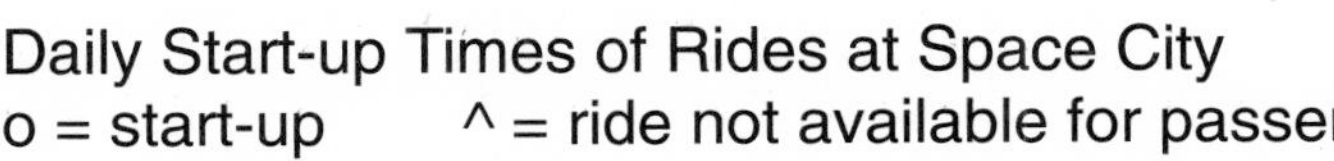

Daily Start-up Times of Rides at Space City
o = start-up ^ = ride not available for passengers

Ride	10 AM	11 AM	Noon	1 PM	2 PM	3 PM
Mercurian Twister	o	^	o	^	^	o
Venusian Link-up	^	^	o	o	^	o
Martian Mayhem	o	o	o	o	o	o
Jupiter's Light Bolt	^	^	o	o	^	o
Ring-Around Saturn	o	^	o	^	o	^
Mist-Stories of Neptune	o	^	o	^	^	^

1. How many times a day does the Mercurian Twister take off? ____________

2. Which ride starts up the most times each day? ____________

3. Which ride starts up the fewest times each day? ____________

4. Which is the only ride to start at 11 AM? ____________

5. If you could not get to the park until 2 PM, which ride would you be unable to take? ____________

6. Which two rides have the same daily schedule? ____________

____

7. The Mercurian Twister ride takes about one hour and fifteen minutes. If you boarded it at 10 AM, would you be able to catch the next Martian Mayhem ride? ____________

8. At which time of day could you choose between all of the six rides? ____________

Time Lines

Read the time line about the life of the writer E. B. White. Then use the information given on the time line to answer the questions that follow it.

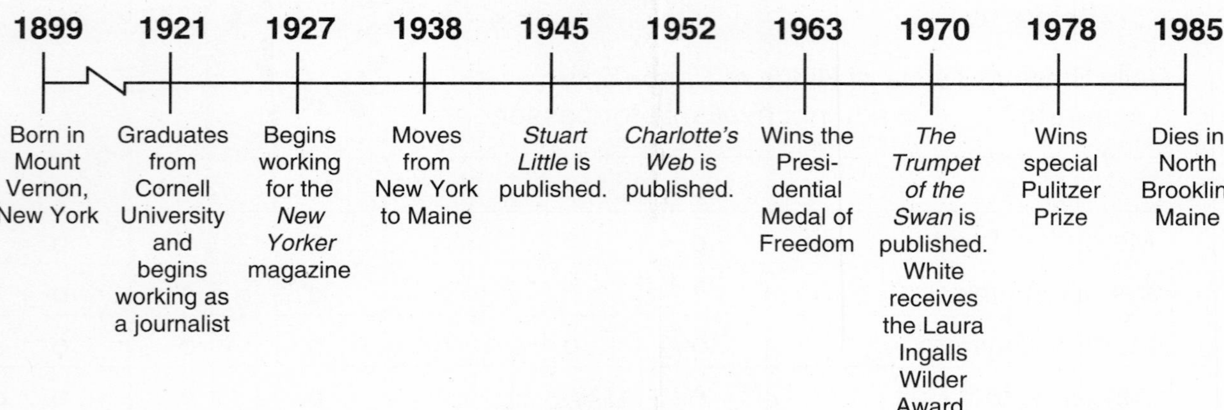

1. When was E. B. White born? ____________________

2. How old was he when he began working for the *New Yorker*? __________

3. Which happened first: White moved to Maine, or *The Trumpet of the Swan* was published? ____________________

4. How many years after *Charlotte's Web* was published did E. B. White win the Presidential Medal of Freedom? ____________________

5. When was E. B. White's book *Stuart Little* published? __________

6. Which happened later: the publication of *Charlotte's Web* or the publication of *The Trumpet of the Swan*? ____________________

____

7. What two events happened in 1970? ____________________

____

____

8. How many years did E. B. White live? ____________________

Choosing Reference Aids

dictionary

telephone directory: white pages

telephone directory: yellow pages

encyclopedia

library card catalog

Write the name of the reference aid shown above that you would use to find the following information.

1. the phone number of the library ______________________
2. the author of the book *Two Bad Ants* ______________________
3. the meaning of the word *quarry* ______________________
4. the titles of books the library has that are written by Byrd Baylor ______________________
5. the address of the electric company ______________________
6. the location of the Pyrenees Mountains ______________________
7. the name of a local car wash ______________________
8. how the word *originate* is divided into syllables ______________________

Now use the reference aid you named to find the information for one of the items listed above.

Locating Information

Skim the selection below by reading the title, the headings, and the first paragraph. Try to get a general idea of what the selection is about.

Everyday Inventions

Many ordinary inventions have their beginnings in everyday life. Here are three examples of good ideas that led to new inventions.

Jigsaw Geography

In 1760, an Englishman named John Spilsbury thought children would learn geography more easily if it were made fun for them. He took a map of England and glued it to a piece of wood. Then he cut the map into pieces and challenged his students to put it back together. Spilsbury's game for teaching geography was the first jigsaw puzzle.

Earmuffs

Fifteen-year-old Chester Greenwood loved ice-skating on the frozen rivers and ponds of his neighborhood in Farmington, Maine. Chester loved skating, but he hated the cold winter wind that made his ears ache. Chester tried tying a scarf around his head, but the scarf would loosen and fall off. Then Chester got an idea. With the help of his grandmother, Chester made what he called "ear protectors." Chester bent a piece of wire and twisted the ends into two hoops. Then his grandmother covered the hoops with cloth. Chester invented his earmuffs in 1873.

Frisbees from Pie Pans

In 1948, Walter Fred Morrison was driving past the Frisbie Pie Company in Bridgeport, Connecticut, when he saw two men throwing pie pans to each other. This gave Morrison an idea. When he returned to his home in Los Angeles, California, he began to make discs shaped like pie pans out of plastic. He then sold the discs at county fairs as "Morrison's Flyin' Saucers." Later the discs were named "Frisbees" after the pie company whose pans had inspired Morrison.

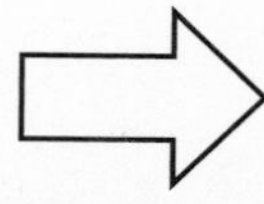

Based on what you have learned by skimming the article, what is the selection about?

____

____

____

Scan the selection to answer the following questions.

1. What did Walter Fred Morrison invent? ______________________________

2. According to the article, what happened in 1873? ______________________________

____

3. How did John Spilsbury teach his students geography? ______________________________

____

____

4. In what state did Walter Fred Morrison first make the "Morrison's Flyin' Saucer"? ______________________________

5. How old was Chester Greenwood when he invented earmuffs?

____

6. What nationality was John Spilsbury? ______________________________

7. In what city and state was the Frisbie Pie Company located? ______________________________

____

8. How did Chester Greenwood's grandmother help him with his invention? ______________________________

9. What were Morrison's first flying discs made out of? ______________________________

____

10. What did Chester Greenwood call his invention? ______________________________

____

11. Where were "Morrison's Flyin' Saucers" first sold? ______________________________

____

Fact and Opinion

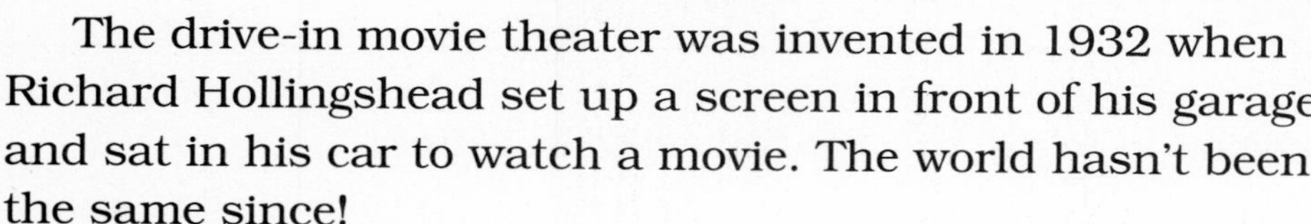

Read the article below.

Motor Movies

The drive-in movie theater was invented in 1932 when Richard Hollingshead set up a screen in front of his garage and sat in his car to watch a movie. The world hasn't been the same since!

Later, Hollingshead set up the world's first public drive-in theater in a vacant lot in Camden, New Jersey. Soon people drove from all over to see movies from their cars.

Hollingshead's idea was so popular that lots of other people began setting up their own drive-in theaters too. They were wrong to copy Hollingshead's idea without asking his permission.

By 1948, there were over 800 drive-ins in America. By 1958, the total had climbed to over 4,000.

Unfortunately, by 1982 the number of drive-in theaters decreased to about 3,500. It's sad that the number of drive-in theaters has gone down. Many people blame the invention of home video equipment for the decrease.

Now read each of the following sentences taken from the passage. Decide whether each sentence is a statement of fact or a statement of opinion. Then write *statement of fact* or *statement of opinion* on the line that follows each sentence.

1. The drive-in movie theater was invented in 1932 when Richard Hollingshead set up a screen in front of his garage and sat in his car to watch a movie. ______________________

2. The world hasn't been the same since! ______________________

3. Later, Hollingshead set up the world's first public drive-in theater in a vacant lot in Camden, New Jersey. ______________________

4. They were wrong to copy Hollingshead's idea without asking his permission. ______________________

5. It's sad that the number of drive-in theaters has gone down. ______________________

Making Outlines

Read the article below.

Ocean Water Temperature and Fish

Ocean water temperature is one of the things that determines what kinds of fish live in what part of the ocean. Many exotic fish can be found in the warm parts of the ocean near the equator. Beautiful fish, such as parrot fish and butterfly fish, are seen there. Dangerous fish, such as the barracuda, live there too.

Away from the equator, the water is temperate. Many fish that are good to eat, such as cod, flatfish, and herring, are plentiful in temperate waters.

The very cold parts of the ocean near the North and South poles have fewer fish. These fish include icefish, eelpouts, and bullheads.

Now complete the outline that follows. Some of the main topics and subtopics have been filled in for you.

Outline of Ocean Water Temperature and Fish

I. **Fish in tropical waters** ______

  A. ______

  B. **Butterfly fish** ______

  C. ______

II. ______

  A. **Cod** ______

  B. ______

  C. ______

III. ______

  A. ______

  B. ______

  C. **Bullheads** ______

Summarizing Information Graphically

Read the article about blood banks below. As you read, think about the problem discussed in the article and how this problem was solved.

Banking Blood

When people give blood to hospitals or to the Red Cross, do you know what happens to it? It is bottled and stored in something called a blood bank. When someone has lost blood and needs some quickly, doctors can often go to a blood bank and get the right type of blood in a matter of minutes.

It was not always as easy as this. In the early 1900's, if a patient needed blood quickly, doctors needed to find the right blood donor immediately.

In most cases, if a donor was found, the blood was transfused directly from the donor to the patient. Whole blood could not be stored for more than a week. Sometimes a donor with the right blood type could not be found immediately. This often meant that the patient needing the blood died.

Dr. Charles Drew felt that a way could be found to store blood for long periods. In 1938, he began research on the subject. By 1940, he discovered that separating plasma—the clear, yellowish fluid part of blood—from whole blood was the answer. Plasma could be stored for long periods. Plasma could also be given to a person of any blood type. The blood banks that Dr. Drew established as a result of his research helped save thousands of lives, especially during World War II when wounded soldiers needed transfusions.

Use what you've learned from the article to complete the problem/solution chart on page 83.

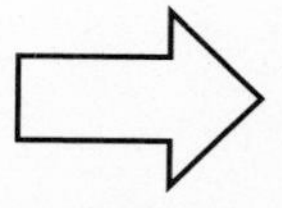

Problem/Solution Chart for *Banking Blood*

Problem: ______________________________

Action: ______________________________

Result: ______________________________

Now that your chart is completed, use it to summarize the article. Write your summary on the lines below.

Banking Blood

K-W-L Strategy

Follow the directions below to help you fill in the K-W-L chart.

1. Think of what you already know about the topic *bird migration.* List two or more facts in the first column of the chart.
2. Survey the article. Then in the column labeled *What I Want to Find Out,* list three things you want to learn from the article about bird migration. Write them as questions.
3. Read the article *Bird Migration* on the next page. As you read, try to find answers to your questions.
4. Now, look over the first two columns of your chart. If you found answers to your questions or details that differed from what you thought you knew, write them in the last column of the chart.

	K-W-L Chart	
What I **K**now	What I **W**ant to Find Out	What I **L**earned

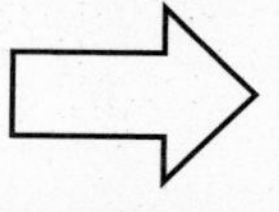

Bird Migration

Have you ever seen a large flock of birds flying in a V-formation? Did you wonder where they were going?

What Migration Is

The birds you saw were probably *migrating.* In science, the word *migrate* means to move from one place to another in large numbers and then to return. Other creatures migrate — fish, elk, and whales — but the migrators that people see and wonder about the most are birds.

Why Birds Migrate

In the fall, as cold weather approaches, plants wither and die. Insects, berries, and seeds begin to disappear. For birds that live where the seasons change, not much food will be left in the coming winter. So in North America most birds fly from north to south to reach a place where the weather is warm and food is plentiful.

Almost a third of the world's birds leave their homes each fall and return in the spring. Some travel thousands of miles without stopping. They stay in their wintering places until spring. Then somehow they know the time has come to return home.

How Birds Know to Migrate

The change of seasons is one reason why birds migrate. As fall approaches, the days become shorter and the nights longer. Scientists believe that the shorter length of daylight tells birds when it is time to migrate.

Shorter daylight hours do not completely explain what starts birds on their journeys, however. Experiments have shown that birds in cages will move to the part of the cage that matches the direction in which they migrate. No matter how the cage is turned or how the amount of daylight is disguised, the birds still move to the correct corner and flutter their wings.

Something inside birds also must tell them to start to migrate. As the days grow shorter, changes take place in birds' bodies. They store extra fat to provide energy for the long trip. Birds also lose their old feathers and grow new ones as their bodies prepare for migration.

Most likely, changes within birds along with seasonal changes outside trigger their urge to migrate.

SQP3R

Survey the article printed below by looking at the map and reading the title, the headings, and the first paragraph. Then answer the questions that follow.

North Island
Tasman Sea
Cook Strait
South Island
Pacific Ocean
Stewart Island
N
E
W
S

New Zealand

Halfway between the equator and the South Pole is the island country of New Zealand. It is in the Pacific Ocean, southeast of Australia, and is about one thousand miles long.

Makeup of the Land

New Zealand is made up of two main islands — North Island and South Island — and a few smaller ones. Snowcapped mountains run down the west coast of South Island.

North Island has mountains, too, but they are not as high as those of South Island. The mountains of North Island are used for grazing sheep and cattle.

Although North Island is the smaller of the two main islands, almost three quarters of the people live there. Cook Strait separates South Island from North Island.

Discovery and Settlement

New Zealand was discovered more than a thousand years ago by people from other Pacific islands. Later, ancestors of the Maori (**MOWR** ee) people who live in New Zealand today came. They continued to arrive until A.D. 1350. In the 1600s, Europeans made their way to New Zealand. In the 1800s, they began to settle there in large numbers.

1. From your survey, what do you think the article is about?

____

____

Return to the section of the article with the heading *Makeup of the Land.* Turn the heading into a question. Then write the question on the line below.

2. Question: ______________________________________

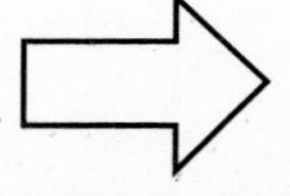

Predict the answer to your question. Write your prediction below.

3. Prediction: ______________________________

____

____

Now read this section of the article. When you have finished the section, write the answer to your question below.

4. Answer: ______________________________

____

____

____

Turn the second heading of the article, *Discovery and Settlement,* into a question. Write the question on the line below.

5. Question: ______________________________

Try to predict the answer to your question. Write your prediction below.

6. Prediction: ______________________________

____

____

Now read this section of the article. When you have finished, write the answer to your question below.

7. Answer: ______________________________

____

____

____

Now cover your answers, and see if you can answer your two questions from memory.

Taking Tests

Complete this page as if it were a test. Pretend that you have fifteen minutes to finish it. Look through the entire test quickly before you begin.

Directions: Answer the question below by writing complete sentences.

1. What steps should you follow when taking any objective test? ______________________________

____

____

____

Directions: Write the letter of the correct answer on the line.

2. __________ In what type of test would you find a question like item 1 above?

a. an objective test b. an essay test c. a matching test

Directions: Match each type of test in the first column with the correct kind of answer in the second column. Write the letter of the answer on the line in front of the type of test.

	Type of Test	Kind of Answer
__________	**3.** essay	a. write T or F
__________	**4.** completion	b. write main ideas and details
__________	**5.** multiple choice	c. choose from answers given
__________	**6.** true–false	d. write words on lines

Directions: Write **T** if the statement is true. Write **F** if it is false.

7. __________ On objective tests, you should try to answer the questions you aren't sure of first.

Directions: Complete the sentence with the name of a type of objective test.

8. In a ______________ test, you must find the item in one column that goes with an item in another column.

PART 2: LANGUAGE ARTS

This Section Provides

- **Writing Center Pages**
- **Language and Usage Lessons**
- **Capitalization, Punctuation, and Usage Guide**

WRITING A STORY

COMPOSITION SKILL: Plot

There are three main parts to a plot. The beginning starts with a problem. The middle tells what happens as a result of the opening situation. The end tells how the problem and its resulting complications are solved.

Think of a story you have read. Write a plot outline of the story. Write only the main points of each part. Leave out the details.

Beginning:

Middle:

End:

WRITING A STORY

COMPOSITION SKILL: Setting and Characters

The setting is the time and the place of a story. The characters are the people, the animals, or the imaginary creatures in a story.

A. Choose one of the story settings below. Write five sentences that show rather than tell about the setting.

1. A forest in North America, long, long ago
2. A shopping mall in the year 2050
3. A city street during a parade or marathon
4. A boat on the ocean during a storm

B. Think of your own setting for a story. Write at least five sentences that show rather than tell about the setting.

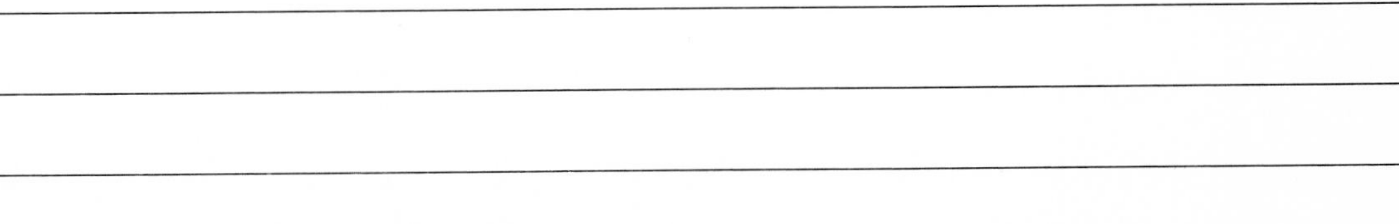

WRITING A STORY

COMPOSITION SKILL: Setting and Characters

C. Choose one of the story settings that you described on page 91. Then think about two characters who might appear in a story with that setting. Describe each character by writing two sentences to answer each question below.

Character 1:

1. What does Character 1 think and do? ______________________

____

____

2. What does Character 1 tell about Character 2? ______________

____

____

Character 2:

3. What does Character 2 think and do? ______________________

____

____

4. What does Character 2 tell about Character 1?

____

____

D. Now write a dialogue between your two characters. Write at least four sentences. Show what each character is like by what each one says.

____

____

____

____

____

____

WRITING A STORY

Revising

Have I	yes
checked that the story has a plot and added to the middle so the plot makes sense?	☐
added details to help describe the setting?	☐
added dialogue to show what the characters are like?	☐
changed the tenses of some verbs so that all verbs are in the same tense?	☐

Revise the following story. Use the check list above to help you. Check off each box when you have finished your revision.

- Use the space above each line, on the sides, and below the story for your changes.

A Very Big Cat

Sam and Eliza were sitting in the park and listening to the radio. Suddenly the music stops, and a news bulletin comes on the radio. A lion had escaped from the park zoo.

Just then they saw the lion coming toward them. They were scared, but Eliza knew what to do. She grabbed Sam's arm and pulled him toward the lake.

When Sam and Eliza arrive home later, Eliza's cat, Itsy, was sitting on the porch. Eliza says, "Good old Itsy. Remember when I tried to give him a bath? Well, it saved our lives!"

Writing a Story

Writing Conference

1. Does the story begin with a problem and end with a solution of the problem?

2. Is the story setting easy to picture?

3. Is dialogue used to bring the characters to life?

WRITING A STORY

Proofreading

Proofreading Marks	
¶	Indent.
∧	Add something.
℘	Take out something.
≡	Capitalize.
/	Make a small letter.

Mrs. Stern didn't call on me. I ~~should of tryed~~ should've tried harder.

Proofread the following paragraphs. There are three spelling errors, four punctuation errors, two run-on sentences, and two mistakes in paragraph format. There are also four errors in capitalization and three errors in forming contractions. Use proofreading marks to correct the mistakes. Use a dictionary to check your spelling.

Carlo was watching Television and feeling sorry for himself. He could of been playing ball. Instead he was stuck in the house. He had to baby-sit for his baby bruther, Daniel. What a bore it was? Suddenly three things happened at once. Daniel cryed, someone pounded at the door, and Carlo smelled smoke. Carlo ran to the door it was his neighbor, Mr Shay.

"Carlo, get out of the house! Its on fire!" Mr. shay yelled. He tried to take Carlo's arm

Carlo pulled away and ran to Daniel's room. smoke filled the room. It was blinding and choking him he grabbed Daniel from the crib. Then he dropped to the floor. The smoke was thinner there. With daniel in one arm, he crawled toard the hall Behind him the room burst into flame.

Carlo flew out the door. The fire engines were just arriving. Carlo hugged his brother. "Im so glad I missed that ball game!" he thought.

WRITING A PERSUASIVE REPORT

COMPOSITION SKILL: Stating and Supporting an Opinion

State your opinion clearly and support it with strong reasons. To persuade others to accept your opinion, give reasons that will appeal to them.

Read each opinion and the two reasons given to support it. Cross out the reason that does not support the opinion well. Then add one reason of your own that would appeal to an audience of your own age.

1. Kids should get allowances only if they do chores.
   a. Doing chores will prepare them for real jobs later on.
   b. Most kids think chores are fun.

____

2. Everyone should get some exercise every day.
   a. Exercise doesn't require any effort.
   b. Exercise helps keep the body strong.

____

3. We must not waste the earth's natural resources.
   a. Natural resources will last forever, no matter what we do.
   b. We cannot survive without our natural resources.

____

4. Everyone should get a good education.
   a. Learning about new things makes life more interesting.
   b. Most people learn enough from watching TV.

____

5. Every city should have a large park.
   a. Natural beauty raises people's spirits.
   b. No one likes living in a city.

____

WRITING A PERSUASIVE REPORT

COMPOSITION SKILL: Ordering Your Reasons

Put reasons for an opinion in an order that will convince your audience, from *most* important to *least* important or from *least* important to *most* important.

Read each of these situations. Follow the directions.

A. You are trying to persuade a friend to take ice skating lessons with you. Write three reasons to convince him or her. Order your reasons from least important to most important.

Reasons: ____

____

____

____

B. You are trying to persuade your classmates to support a recycling program at school. Write three reasons to convince them. Order your reasons from most important to least important.

Reasons: ____

____

____

____

C. You are trying to persuade your parents to let you spend the summer on your aunt and uncle's farm. Write three reasons to convince them. Order your reasons from least important to most important.

Reasons: ____

____

____

____

WRITING A PERSUASIVE REPORT

Revising

Have I | **yes**

- rewritten the topic sentence so that it clearly states the opinion? ☐
- rewritten weak reasons to make them stronger and crossed out reasons that do not support the opinion? ☐
- added reasons that will be convincing to the audience? ☐
- arranged the reasons in order from most important to least important? ☐

Revise the following persuasive report. Check off each box above when you have finished your revision.

- Use the space above each line, on the sides, and below.

Do you know how to swim? Swimming is good for your health. Learning a new sport helps give you confidence, too. You will be proud to see your skills improve. I can do the crawl, the breast stroke, and the back stroke. Swimming does not have to be expensive, either. You can usually swim in a public pool or at a community center for just a small fee. Being able to swim can save your life or help you save someone else's life.

Writing a Persuasive Report

Writing Conference

1. Are the ideas well supported with reasons?
2. Are the reasons stated in the best order?
3. Are there parts that could be made stronger by adding details or persuasive words?

WRITING A PERSUASIVE REPORT

Proofreading

When you proofread, look for mistakes in spelling, capitalization, and punctuation. Use proofreading marks to make corrections.

every young ~~persen~~ person ~~shoud~~ should have a Pet?.

Proofreading Marks	
¶	Indent.
∧	Add something.
℘	Take out something.
≡	Capitalize.
/	Make a small letter.

Proofread this persuasive report. Find five mistakes in capitalization, three spelling errors, one run-on sentence, and one mistake in paragraph format. There are four errors in punctuation. Correct the mistakes. Use a dictionary to check your spelling.

I think that some of the walls at Booker T. washington Elementary School should have murals painted on them. The hallways are very dull murals would make them more interesting. The Murals could be educational, too? They could show important events in histery or different jobs people do. All the subjecs that we study could be included in some way, Many students in this school have talent in art, The art teachers, Mrs. franzioni and Mr Kemp, could help them design and paint the murals. these students would be learning a new skil and making our School look better too. We would all enjoy the results.

WRITING — HISTORICAL EVENT

COMPOSITION SKILL: Identifying Cause and Effect

To figure out the cause of an event, ask *Why did it happen?* To figure out the effect of an event, ask *What happened as a result?*

A. Read the paragraph and then answer the questions below.

The pony express, which carried mail to California in a system of horse-and-rider relays, lasted only about nineteen months. The need for the service ended when the coast-to-coast telegraph system was completed in 1861. The telegraph delivered messages more quickly and cheaply. The pony express offices closed two days after the telegraph system opened.

1. What cause or causes are stated in the paragraph?

____

____

2. What effect or effects are stated?

____

____

B. Write two possible effects of the weather on a mail service that depended on horses and riders.

____

____

____

____

C. Write two possible causes of the loss of more than $100,000 by the pony express company during its operation.

____

____

____

____

WRITING — HISTORICAL EVENT

COMPOSITION SKILL: Sequence of Events

Describe events in a logical sequence, or order. Use order words, such as *first, after, when,* and *while,* to make the sequence clear.

Read this paragraph and then follow the directions below.

The year was 1804. The 45 people in the Lewis and Clark expedition first sailed up the Missouri River into what is now North Dakota. After a while they found a suitable place to spend the winter, and there they built a small fort. When spring came, the explorers continued their journey up the river. After they acquired horses from a band of Shoshone, the expedition crossed the Rocky Mountains. Finally, in 1805, they reached the Pacific Ocean. A year and a half had passed.

1. Where did the explorers travel first? ______________________________

____

2. When did they continue up the Missouri from North Dakota? ______________________________

3. What order words are used in this paragraph? ____________________

____

4. List the events in order.

____

____

____

____

____

____

____

____

____

____

WRITING — HISTORICAL EVENT

COMPOSITION SKILL: Using Descriptive Language

When you write about a historical event, use interesting details. Some details will come from your research. Even details from your imagination must be historically accurate.

Not enough detail: Alexander Graham Bell presented his new invention.

Not historically accurate: Alexander Graham Bell presented his new invention on a TV program. (Bell lived from 1847 to 1922; experiments with television began in 1923.)

Interesting detail: Alexander Graham Bell presented his new invention — the world's first telephone — at the Centennial Exhibition in Philadelphia in June, 1876.

Read the pairs of details below. They are possible details for describing Chief Joseph, who lived from 1840 to 1904, and the struggle of his people, the Nez Percé. Put a check beside the more interesting detail in each pair or beside the one that seems more appropriate for the historical period.

1. _____ The Nez Percé were ordered to move to reservation lands.
_____ The government ordered Chief Joseph's band to move from its homeland in Oregon to a reservation in Idaho.

2. _____ The government wanted land opened to white settlers.
_____ The government wanted the land to establish an air base.

3. _____ Chief Joseph said he would go.
_____ Chief Joseph reluctantly agreed.

4. _____ Then trouble started.
_____ Then young Nez Percé killed some white settlers.

5. _____ The Nez Percé fled in any car or truck they could find.
_____ Fearing revenge, the Nez Percé fled.

6. _____ They tried to reach Canada.
_____ TV cameras followed their flight north.

7. _____ Chief Joseph led the band over 1000 difficult miles.
_____ It was a long, hard trip.

8. _____ Cold and starvation took many lives.
_____ Many people died.

WRITING — HISTORICAL EVENT

Revising

Have I	**yes**
described the historical event and its causes accurately?	☐
arranged the facts in the correct order?	☐
used enough historical details to make my story seem true to life?	☐
checked the accuracy of my historical details?	☐

Revise the following story about a historical event. Use the check list above to help you. Check off each box when you have finished your revision.

- Use the space above each line, on the sides, and below the story for your changes.

The California Gold Rush

On January 24, 1848, a man named James Marshall discovered several nuggets of gold at Sutter's Mill in Oregon. The next year, thousands of "Forty-Niners" came to California from all over the world. They hoped to find gold. News of his discovery spread over the radio and TV. This started the greatest gold rush in U.S. history. Within a year, San Francisco grew from a small town to a city. Not everyone got rich. Some went home poor. Some stayed on.

WRITING — HISTORICAL EVENT

Writing Conference

1. Are the important causes and effects described?
2. Are order words used so that the order of events is clear?
3. Are the details historically accurate?

WRITING — HISTORICAL EVENT

Proofreading

amelia Earhart ~~tryd~~ tried to fly around the ~~wurld~~ world

Proofreading Marks	
¶	Indent.
^	Add something.
ℓ	Take out something.
≡	Capitalize.
/	Make a small letter.

Proofread this story about historical events. Find three mistakes in capitalization, three spelling errors, one double negative, and one mistake in verb tense (use past tense instead of present). There are two errors in punctuation. Correct the mistakes. Use a dictionary to check your spelling.

Major Flights of Amelia Earhart

On june 18 1928, Amelia Earhart became famous wen she flew across the Atlantic ocean in an airplane. She was only a passenger, but she was the first women to make such a flight? Four years later, she made history again. She flew the same route all by herself. In 1935 Earhart became the first person to fly from Hawaii to califor-nia. Then, in 1937, she and navigator Fred Noonan take off to fly around the world. After they stoped to refuel their plane, they head-ed for Howland Island. No one never saw them again.

WRITING A PERSONAL NARRATIVE

COMPOSITION SKILL: Writing a Good Beginning

Poor Beginning: I learned to roller-skate when I was seven.
Better Beginning: They called me the eight-wheeled terror.

A. Write two good beginnings for each of the stories below. Put a check next to the one you like better.

1. . . . I sat down in the back of the classroom and hoped nobody would notice me. Everyone else was talking and laughing and catching up on weekend news. I closed my eyes and tried to imagine I was back in my old school. Why did we have to move?

Beginning: ______________________________

____

Beginning: ______________________________

____

2. . . . Mrs. Liu was on the phone. I told her my brother Oscar was at soccer practice and couldn't baby-sit that afternoon. I was surprised when she asked me if I could do it instead. "Sure," I said, but I wasn't sure at all. Would I know what to do?

Beginning: ______________________________

____

Beginning: ______________________________

____

B. Think of a funny, sad, or frightening experience that you have had or have observed. Write two good beginnings for a story about what happened. Put a check next to the better beginning.

Beginning: ______________________________

____

Beginning: ______________________________

____

WRITING A PERSONAL NARRATIVE

COMPOSITION SKILL: Supplying Details

Poor Detail: I was cold.
Interesting Detail: My toes were aching and my teeth were chattering by the time the bus arrived.

Read the following paragraphs. Then rewrite each paragraph, adding details to make each one more interesting.

A. It was easy to see that a birthday party had taken place. The table was covered with leftovers. Wrapping paper and other things were scattered around the room. Decorations hung from the walls and ceiling.

B. It was the top of the eighth inning, and the score was tied. It was my turn at bat. I stepped up to the plate. The crowd made a lot of noise. Everyone was looking at me. I was so nervous. What would I do?

WRITING A PERSONAL NARRATIVE

COMPOSITION SKILL: Writing Dialogue

> "What is dialogue in a story?" asked Mr. Mayo.
> Hoshi replied, "It's the exact words of the characters."

A. Rewrite the sentences below as dialogue. Put quotation marks around the exact words that each person might say. Try to make the dialogue sound the way people really talk.

Mom told me to set the table. I asked whether it was my turn. She said no, but Ronald was at a rehearsal. I agreed to do it if Ronald would be my slave for a month.

____

____

____

____

____

B. Look at the illustration below. Write dialogue between the two characters.

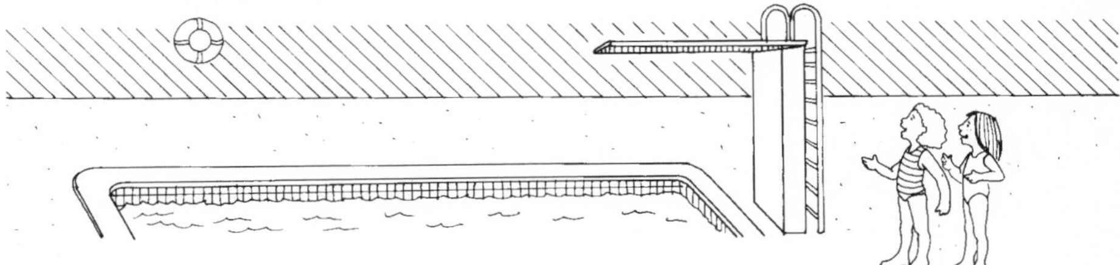

Write at least two sentences for each character.

____

____

____

____

____

____

WRITING A PERSONAL NARRATIVE

COMPOSITION SKILL: Writing a Good Title

Poor Title: The Time I Was on Television
Good Title: Why I'll Never Be a TV Star

Read each story below. Write two good titles for each one. Underline the title that you like better in each pair.

A. ______________________________

____

When Pip wandered into my yard, it was love at first sight. Don't ask me why. He wasn't great looking. A collie's nose, a cocker spaniel's ears, and a poodle's fur don't go all that well together. He wasn't very smart, either. Still, he showed up when I needed a friend, and a friend he truly was.

B. ______________________________

____

Last summer I saw the ocean for the first time. I had seen it in pictures and movies, of course, but the real thing was better than I ever imagined. I loved taking long walks on the wet sand, with the sun warming my back and the cool waves splashing my bare feet. Most of all, I loved the treasures I found along the way.

C. ______________________________

____

The talent show was two weeks away, and I still hadn't thought of anything to do. I couldn't sing or play an instrument. I couldn't dance or do gymnastics. Then I had an idea. I dug into a box of junk in my closet and pulled out a tattered book — *1000 Jokes for Kids.* "I'll be a stand-up comic!" I decided.

Writing a Personal Narrative

Revising

Have I **yes**

- changed the beginning so that it will catch a reader's attention? ☐
- added details that give a clear picture? ☐
- added dialogue that brings the characters to life? ☐
- written an interesting title that does not tell too much? ☐

Revise the following story. Check off each box above when you have finished your revision.

- Use the space above each line, on the sides, and below the paragraph for your changes.

A Great Costume

My friend Rosa and I were invited to a Halloween party, and there was going to be a prize for the best costume. We were discussing what to wear. Then I had a brilliant idea. We could go as a two-headed robot.

We cut two holes in a sheet and sewed up the sides. We decorated the sheet in a crazy way and made weird-looking things for our heads. Then we walked in a funny way and used some strange sounds for our "language."

We won first prize! We were very happy.

Writing a Personal Narrative

Writing Conference

1. Does the story begin in an interesting way?

2. Are there enough details to make the story clear?

3. Has dialogue been used to add interest?

4. Does the story have a good title?

WRITING A PERSONAL NARRATIVE

Proofreading

night fire
the nite was cold but the fier was warm.

Proofreading Marks

- ¶ Indent.
- ∧ Add something.
- Take out something.
- ≡ Capitalize.
- / Make a small letter.

A. Proofread the following story. Find three mistakes in spelling, one mistake in capitalization, one missing end mark, one run-on sentence, and one mistake in a compound sentence. Use proofreading marks to correct the mistakes. Use a dictionary to check your spelling.

My favrite uncle, Patrick, has an unusual job He sets up a chair and easel on the sidewalk. Then he draws people's faces the people pay him eight dollers. He draws very quickly and the drawings look just like the people. Every year Patrick comes to my birtday party and draws my friends. then they can take home pictures of themselves.

B. Proofread this story. There are four mistakes in spelling, one mistake in end punctuation, and one mistake in a compound sentence. Correct the mistakes.

I was standing near a bush when something colorfull caught my eye. I turned my head and saw an amazeing sight. It was a tiny green bird with a red throat? Its beak lookd like a needle. Its wings were moving very fast and it just hung in the air. I had seen my furst hummingbird!

WRITING A RESEARCH REPORT

COMPOSITION SKILL: Finding Facts

A **dictionary** gives spellings, pronunciations, and meanings of words.
An **encyclopedia** gives basic information about many subjects.
An **almanac** contains articles, lists, tables, and recent information.
An **atlas** contains maps and tables of information about places.
Newspapers and **magazines** contain up-to-date information.
Nonfiction books give facts about real people, places, and events.

Write *dictionary, encyclopedia, almanac, atlas, newspaper, magazine,* or *nonfiction book* to tell where to find the answer to each question.

1. What is the definition of the word *satellite*? ____________________
2. When was the first satellite launched? ____________________
3. Where is Cape Canaveral? ____________________
4. How many space flights have there been? ____________________
5. How are satellites used in predicting weather? ____________________ ____________________
6. What is the weather forecast for tomorrow? ____________________
7. How is the word *satellite* pronounced? ____________________
8. Was yesterday's space launch successful? ____________________
9. What is Neil Armstrong most famous for? ____________________
10. How did Neil Armstrong become an astronaut? ____________________ ____________________
11. What role does the Lyndon B. Johnson Space Center play in space travel? ____________________
12. How far is Houston, Texas, from Cape Canaveral? ____________________
13. Who were the crew members of the space shuttle last year? ____________________
14. What is life like on a space shuttle? ____________________

WRITING A RESEARCH REPORT

COMPOSITION SKILL: Taking Notes

Take notes to help you remember what you have read. Write down **key words** that will help you recall information. Include all important facts and use your own words.

Read the paragraph below. Then write notes to answer the question that follows.

Penguin fathers play an important role in caring for their young. After a mother lays an egg, she leaves for the sea, and the father takes over. He rolls the egg onto his feet and uses the lower part of his belly to keep it warm. With the egg on his feet, he waddles into a large group with other penguin fathers. The fathers huddle together for warmth. They remain that way for two months, without eating. When a chick hatches, the father feeds it a milklike food that he produces in his throat. Soon, the mother penguin returns. The father then goes to sea. In three weeks he returns with food for the chick.

What role do penguin fathers play in caring for their young?

WRITING A RESEARCH REPORT

COMPOSITION SKILL: Making an Outline

Make an outline from your notes by writing the questions as the **main topics**. Place each main topic after a Roman numeral and a period. List supporting facts as **subtopics**. Place each subtopic after a capital letter and a period. The first word of a main topic or subtopic starts with a capital letter. Give your outline a title.

Write an outline, using the notes below. Rewrite the questions as main topics. Rewrite the notes that answer the questions as subtopics. Put the subtopics in an order that makes sense. Give your outline a title.

What are some facts about Mother Teresa's background?
— at age 40, began the Missionaries of Charity
— was born in 1910 in what became Yugoslavia
— at 18, joined a religious order in Yugoslavia

What work does the Missionaries of Charity do?
— supplies food to the needy
— runs hospitals
— sets up schools, orphanages, and youth centers
— provides shelter for needy people with incurable illnesses

Title: ______________________________

I. ______________________________

A. ______________________________

B. ______________________________

C. ______________________________

II. ______________________________

A. ______________________________

B. ______________________________

C. ______________________________

D. ______________________________

WRITING A RESEARCH REPORT

COMPOSITION SKILL: Writing a Paragraph from an Outline

Each section of an outline is about one main idea. When you write a paragraph from an outline section, think about the main idea to write a topic sentence for the paragraph. Then use the subtopics to write supporting details in complete sentences.

Write a paragraph from each of the following outline sections. Write a good topic sentence. Write the supporting details in the subtopics in complete sentences.

The Seven Wonders of the Ancient World

I. The Colossus of Rhodes
- **A.** Huge bronze statue
- **B.** Honored the sun god Helios
- **C.** Stood about 120 feet tall
- **D.** Built by Greek sculptor Chares
- **E.** Took 12 years to build

____

____

____

____

Peanut

I. How it grows
- **A.** Fruit of peanut plant
- **B.** Not a nut but a kind of pea
- **C.** Two peanuts in each pod, or shell
- **D.** Unusual plant because pods grow under the ground

____

____

____

____

WRITING A RESEARCH REPORT

Revising

Have I	**yes**
replaced the weak opening with an interesting one?	☐
written a topic sentence for the paragraph?	☐
combined facts to make a sentence more interesting and moved one fact so that the order makes sense?	☐
replaced unclear pronouns and added details to make a sentence clearer?	☐

Revise the following paragraph from a research report. Check off each box above when you have finished.

- Use the space above each line, on the sides, and below.
- Use the outline section below to write a topic sentence and to check that all the facts have been used in the paragraph.

I. How the Peace Corps helps others
  A. American men and women volunteer
  B. Volunteers selected and trained
  C. Serve for two years
  D. Sent to countries that ask for help
  E. Usually go to small villages
  F. Try to improve farming, health care, education

This report is about the Peace Corps. Most of the projects help people in villages. American men and women can volunteer. The Peace Corps selects and trains them. Volunteers serve for two years. They are sent to countries that have requested help. They try to improve farming, health care, and education.

WRITING A RESEARCH REPORT

Writing Conference

1. Are there enough interesting facts about the topic?
2. Do the paragraphs follow the outline of the report?
3. Do the sentences in each paragraph support the main idea?
4. Does the closing sum up the main ideas in the report?

WRITING A RESEARCH REPORT

Proofreading

afraid
are You affraid of bats?

Proofreading Marks

- ¶ Indent.
- ^ Add something.
- Take out something.
- ≡ Capitalize.
- / Make a small letter.

Proofread the following report. There are three spelling errors, five capitalization errors, and one mistake in paragraph format. There are two punctuation errors and two run-on sentences. There are three mistakes in the use of pronouns. Use proofreading marks to correct the errors. Use a dictionary to check your spelling.

the Bat

Is it a mouse with wings? Is it a bird with pointed ears and a snout. No, it is a bat. The bat is a strange-looking animal it has a furry body and leathery wings. The bat's head looks like that of a dog or a bare, and they has tiny, sharp teeth. Bats have unusual habits. during the day them sleep in places like caves and attics, hanging upside down by their fete. As evening comes, they fly from its roosts to find Food. A bat may eat half its weight in food every nit. Most bats in North america eat insects how does the bat find its food? It makes high sounds that echo off objects The echoes tell the Bat where an object is.

Four Kinds of Sentences

There are four kinds of sentences. Each kind does a different job. All four kinds begin with a capital letter. The end mark varies, however.

Declarative: A **declarative sentence** tells something. It ends with a period.	**W**hales are mammals**.**
Interrogative: An **interrogative sentence** asks something. It ends with a question mark.	**D**o you like whales**?**
Imperative: An **imperative sentence** gives an order. It ends with a period.	**W**atch them dive**.**
Exclamatory: An **exclamatory sentence** expresses strong feeling. It ends with an exclamation point.	**H**ow big they are**!** **T**hey are so big**!**

Guided Practice

Identify each sentence as *declarative, interrogative, imperative,* or *exclamatory.* Which end punctuation would you use?

Example: Can whales dive very deep
interrogative ***question mark***

1. Some whales dive down half a mile
2. How deep that is
3. The whales stay underwater a long time
4. Do they need any air
5. Read this article for information

REMINDER

- A **declarative sentence** tells something. It ends with a period *(.)*.
- An **interrogative sentence** asks a question. It ends with a question mark *(?)*.
- An **imperative sentence** gives an order. It ends with a period *(.)*.
- An **exclamatory sentence** shows strong feeling. It ends with an exclamation point *(!)*.

Declarative Sentence:	**W**hales rise to the surface of the water**.**
Interrogative Sentence:	**D**o they breathe air**?**
Imperative Sentence:	**T**ell me about their songs**.**
Exclamatory Sentence:	**I** cannot imagine that**!**

INDEPENDENT PRACTICE

Write each sentence. Add the correct end punctuation. The kind of sentence is shown in parentheses.

Example: Mammals must breathe to live **(declarative)**
Mammals must breathe to live.

1. Can whales hold their breath **(interrogative)**

2. Some whales hold their breath more than an hour **(declarative)**

3. Think about that amount of time **(imperative)**

4. That is more than sixty minutes **(exclamatory)**

5. How much food does the whale find underwater **(interrogative)**

Combining Sentences: Compound Subjects

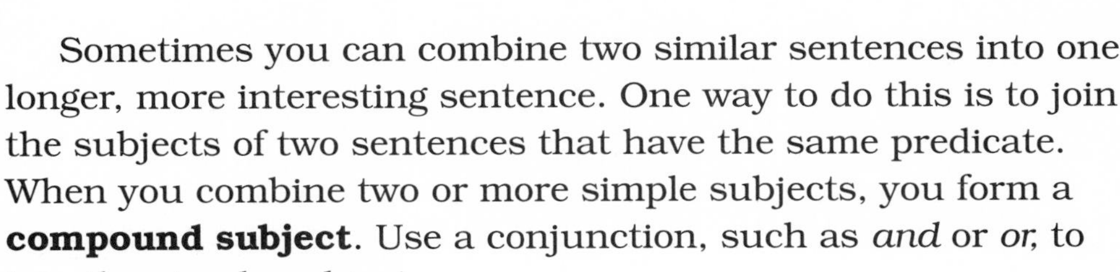

Sometimes you can combine two similar sentences into one longer, more interesting sentence. One way to do this is to join the subjects of two sentences that have the same predicate. When you combine two or more simple subjects, you form a **compound subject**. Use a conjunction, such as *and* or *or,* to join the simple subjects.

Rabbits had left tracks.
Foxes had left tracks.
→ **Rabbits** or **foxes** had left tracks.

Gloria saw the footprints.
Felipe saw the footprints.
A **friend** saw the footprints.
→ **Gloria, Felipe,** and a **friend** saw the footprints.

Guided Practice

Combine each pair of sentences by forming a compound subject. Use the conjunction *and.*

Example: Meg followed the tracks.
Her aunt followed the tracks.
Meg and her aunt followed the tracks.

1. Roni stayed on the path.
Bob stayed on the path.

____

2. Sights were mysterious.
Sounds were mysterious.

____

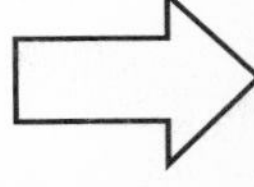

REMINDER

- A **compound subject** is two or more simple subjects that have the same predicate. Use a conjunction, such as *and* or *or,* to join simple subjects.

  Simple Subjects: **Ty** saw a nature series on television.
  His **dad** saw a nature series on television.

  Compound Subject: **Ty** and his **dad** saw a nature series on television.

INDEPENDENT PRACTICE

Find the compound subject in each sentence. Write the simple subjects joined by each underlined conjunction.

Example: Many birds and other animals survive in cities.
birds, animals

1. Ducks and geese swim in park ponds.

   ____

2. Hawks and pigeons make nests on tall buildings.

   ____

3. Small chipmunks, squirrels, and mice often eat birdseed.

   ____

4. Wild moose or deer appear in some cities.

   ____

5. Some foxes, skunks, or raccoons raid trash cans.

   ____

6. Buildings, bridges, or unused chimneys protect many animals.

   ____

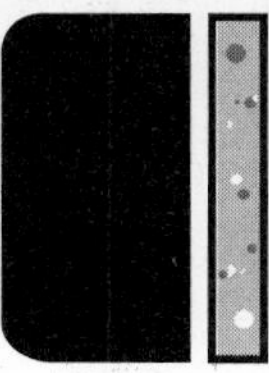

Combining Sentences: Compound Predicates

You have learned how to join the subjects of two sentences to form a new sentence. You can also combine the predicates of sentences that have the same subject. When you join two or more simple predicates, you form a **compound predicate**. Use a conjunction, such as *and* or *or*, to join the simple predicates.

The twigs **bend**.
The twigs **break**.
→ The twigs **bend** and **break**.

Carla **saw** the plants.
Carla **recognized** the plants.
Carla **named** the plants.
→ Carla **saw, recognized,** and **named** the plants.

Guided Practice

A. What is the compound predicate in each sentence? What conjunction joins the simple predicates?

Example: Harmful plants grow and spread.
grow and spread ***conjunction:*** *and*

1. Some plants harm or poison people.
2. My class found and identified several plants.
3. We examined, compared, and labeled each one.
4. Our teacher watched us or helped.

B. Combine each pair of sentences by forming a compound predicate. Use the conjunction *and*.

Example: Some leaves shone. Some leaves glistened.
Some leaves shone and glistened.

5. The hikers stopped. The hikers looked.

____

6. The leader noticed the plant. The leader named the plant.

____

REMINDER

- A **compound predicate** is two or more simple predicates that have the same subject. Use a conjunction, such as *and* or *or*, to join simple predicates.

Simple Predicates: Kim **saw** the poison ivy.
Kim **avoided** the poison ivy.

Compound Predicate: Kim **saw** and **avoided** the poison ivy.

INDEPENDENT PRACTICE

Find the compound predicate in each sentence. Write the simple predicates joined by each underlined conjunction.

Example: Poison ivy attacks and irritates the skin.
attacks, irritates

1. The ivy vine climbed and spread.

2. Will touched the leaves or bumped against them.

3. Oils stayed on his skin and irritated it.

4. His legs blistered, burned, or itched.

5. Will rubbed or scratched his legs.

6. Mom called the doctor and explained.

7. Dr. Randall looked, sighed, and applied a lotion.

8. Now Will wears long pants or washes his legs after hiking.

Run-on Sentences

A **run-on sentence** is two or more sentences that are run together incorrectly. One way that you can correct a run-on sentence is to make it into a compound sentence.

The frog jumped. It landed in the pond.

RUN-ON: Many tourists visit famous caves these places amaze people.

CORRECTED: Many tourists visit famous caves, and these places amaze people.

To correct a run-on that has three parts, try dividing it into one compound sentence and one short sentence.

RUN-ON: A park in Kentucky attracts tourists the visitors travel through a huge cave they see an underground river.

CORRECTED: A park in Kentucky attracts tourists. *(short)* The visitors travel through a huge cave, and they see an underground river. *(compound)*

Another way to correct a run-on sentence is to divide it into separate sentences.

RUN-ON: Strange creatures live inside the cave the fish have no eyes.

CORRECTED: Strange creatures live inside the cave. The fish have no eyes.

Guided Practice

How would you correct these run-on sentences?

Example: The climate inside is cool the cave is moist.
The climate inside is cool. The cave is moist.

1. The park offers tours some tours are short.
2. One tour lasts six hours many people avoid it.
3. Our visit to the cave was an adventure the tour was two hours long it seemed too short.

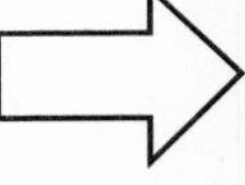

REMINDER

- A **run-on sentence** is two or more sentences that are put together incorrectly. Correct a run-on sentence by making separate sentences or by making a compound sentence.

  Run-on Sentence: Mammoth Cave is 194 miles long it is the longest cave.

  Correct: Mammoth Cave is 194 miles long**.** **I**t is the longest cave.

  Also Correct: Mammoth Cave is 194 miles long, and it is the longest cave.

INDEPENDENT PRACTICE

Correct each run-on sentence by writing it as two separate sentences.

Example: A river flows below the surface there are odd fish in it.

A river flows below the surface. There are odd fish in it.

1. The fish have no eyes they are also colorless.

____

2. The cave has five levels some paths are not mapped.

____

3. Visit Mammoth Cave in Kentucky it is part of a national park.

____

4. The park also has forests the area covers many miles.

____

5. Prehistoric people first entered the cave some remains have been found.

____

____

6. The cave gets its name from extinct animals once mammoths roamed there.

____

____

Plural Nouns

Some nouns do not become plural according to the regular rules of adding *s* or *es*. There are, however, patterns that will help you remember how to form the plurals of these nouns. The chart below groups some of these nouns according to their patterns. You can also use your dictionary to find the plural spellings of nouns.

More Rules for Forming Plurals		
1.	**Nouns ending in *f* or *fe*:** Change the *f* to *v* and add *es* to some nouns. Add *s* to other nouns.	wolf — wol**ves** wife — wi**ves** staff — staff**s** roof — roof**s**
2.	**Nouns ending with a vowel and *o*:** Add *s*.	stereo — stereo**s** igloo — igloo**s** radio — radio**s**
3.	**Nouns ending with a consonant and *o*:** Add *s* to some nouns. Add *es* to other nouns.	piano — piano**s** solo — solo**s** mosquito — mosquito**es** hero — hero**es** potato — potato**es**
4.	**Nouns that have special plural spellings**	tooth — t**ee**th child — child**ren**
5.	**Nouns that remain the same in the singular and the plural**	moose — moose deer — deer sheep — sheep

GUIDED PRACTICE

What is the plural form of each noun? You may use your dictionary to help you.

Example: echo *echoes*

1. foot
2. calf
3. sheep
4. tomato
5. knife
6. radio
7. giraffe
8. cliff
9. hero

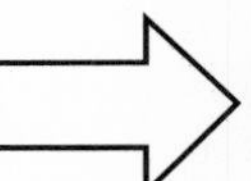

REMINDER

	Singular	Plural
• To form the plural of some nouns ending in *f* or *fe*, change the *f* to *v* and add *es*.	lea_f_	lea**ves**
• For other nouns ending in *f* or *fe*, add *s*.	clif_f_	cliff**s**
• To form the plural of nouns ending in *o*, add *s* or *es*.	rode_o_	rodeo**s**
	ech_o_	echo**es**
• Some nouns have special plural spellings.	man	m**e**n
• Some nouns have the same singular and plural forms.	trout	trout

INDEPENDENT PRACTICE

Write the plural form of each singular noun in parentheses. You may use your dictionary.

Example: some **men** **(man)**

1. many ______________ **(sheep)**
2. these ______________ **(thief)**
3. five ______________ **(roof)**
4. six ______________ **(elk)**
5. all ______________ **(igloo)**
6. these ______________ **(wife)**
7. fifty ______________ **(tomato)**
8. some ______________ **(soprano)**
9. many ______________ **(knife)**
10. both ______________ **(chief)**
11. seven ______________ **(woman)**
12. those ______________ **(giraffe)**
13. few ______________ **(radio)**
14. ten ______________ **(ox)**
15. all ______________ **(cliff)**
16. many ______________ **(studio)**
17. two ______________ **(foot)**
18. three ______________ **(potato)**
19. some ______________ **(leaf)**
20. four ______________ **(stereo)**
21. these ______________ **(calf)**
22. nine ______________ **(life)**
23. twelve ______________ **(deer)**
24. those ______________ **(cuff)**
25. both ______________ **(child)**
26. eight ______________ **(video)**
27. many ______________ **(tooth)**
28. three ______________ **(wolf)**

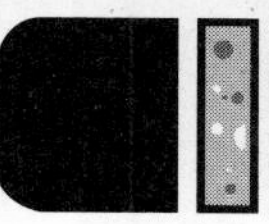
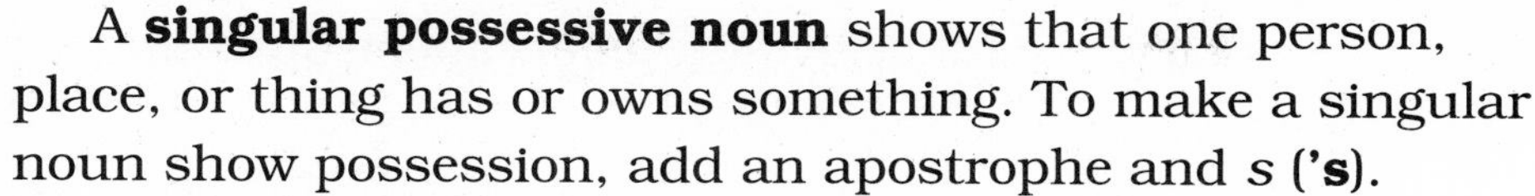

Singular Possessive Nouns

A **singular possessive noun** shows that one person, place, or thing has or owns something. To make a singular noun show possession, add an apostrophe and *s* (**'s**).

the spoon **of the cook**	the **cook's** spoon
the paper **that the teacher has**	the **teacher's** paper

Using possessive nouns is shorter and better than other ways of showing possession.

LONGER: The hat **that belongs to the miner** is heavy.
BETTER: The **miner's** hat is heavy.

Singular noun	**Singular possessive noun**
man	man'**s** uniform
Jess	Jess'**s** truck
puppy	puppy'**s** bone
deer	deer'**s** eyes

GUIDED PRACTICE

Each phrase can be changed to show possession in a shorter way. What is the possessive form of each underlined singular noun?

Example: the chair of the dentist
the ________ chair *dentist's*

1. the whistle of the lifeguard
the ________ whistle

2. the phone of the detective
the ________ phone

3. the key that Rex has
________ key

4. the mitt of the catcher
the ________ mitt

5. the badge that Lucy has
________ badge

6. the scarf my aunt owns
my ________ scarf

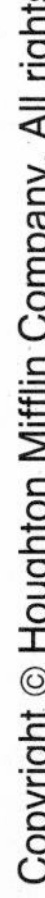

Reminder

- A **singular possessive noun** shows that one person, place, or thing has or owns something.
- Form a singular possessive noun by adding an apostrophe and *s* **('s)** to a singular noun.

Singular nouns	Singular possessive nouns
child	**child's** toys
Les	**Les's** trip
monkey	**monkey's** tail

Independent Practice

Write each sentence correctly by making the underlined noun possessive.

Example: Molly was voted the team best goalie.
Molly was voted the team's best goalie.

1. Roberto school paper announces the news.

2. His best friend sister writes the story.

3. Molly dream is the state championship.

4. Her family help was important.

5. Her mother face shows joy.

6. Uncle Jess phone call is very welcome.

7. He had predicted his niece success.

8. Her father gift of roses makes the day complete.

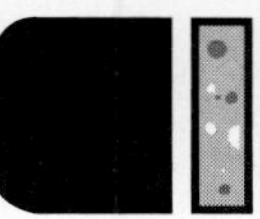

Plural Possessive Nouns

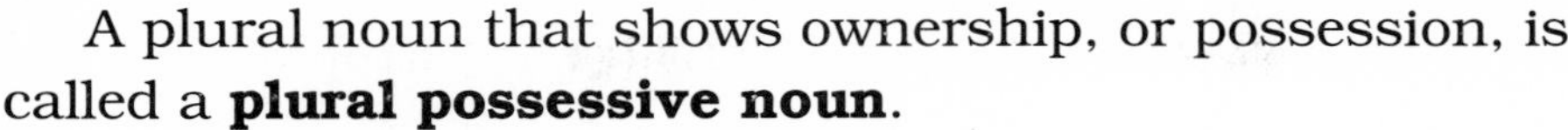

A plural noun that shows ownership, or possession, is called a **plural possessive noun**.

The maps **that belong to the guides** are old.
The **guides'** maps are old.

When a plural noun ends in *s*, add only an apostrophe after the *s* to make the noun show possession.

owl**s'** eyes   calve**s'** barn   fireflie**s'** wings

Not all plural nouns end in *s*. When a plural noun does not end in *s*, add **'s** to form the plural possessive noun.

the toys **of the children**   the **children's** toys
the bells **of the sheep**   the **sheep's** bells
the feathers **of the geese**   the **geese's** feathers

Singular	**Singular possessive**	**Plural**	**Plural possessive**
girl	girl's	girls	girls'
calf	calf's	calves	calves'
pony	pony's	ponies	ponies'
child	child's	children	children's
mouse	mouse's	mice	mice's
deer	deer's	deer	deer's

GUIDED PRACTICE

How would you change each phrase to show possession?

Example: nurses__ uniforms   *nurses' uniforms*

1. elephants__ tusks
2. classes__ books
3. students__ names
4. golfers__ clubs
5. people__ habits
6. porcupines__ quills

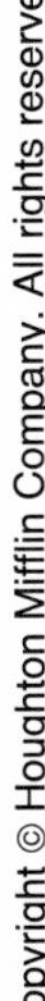

REMINDER

- A **plural possessive noun** shows that more than one person, place, or thing has or owns something.
- Form a plural possessive noun by adding an apostrophe *(')* to a plural noun that ends with *s*. Add an apostrophe and *s* *('s)* to a plural noun that does not end with *s*.

Plural Nouns	Plural Possessive Nouns
girls	**girls'** clothes
foxes	**foxes'** ears
puppies	**puppies'** tails
men	**men's** desks
moose	**moose's** calves

INDEPENDENT PRACTICE

The underlined word in each sentence is not correct. Rewrite each sentence so that it includes a plural possessive noun.

Example: The men questions about the camp were answered.
The men's questions about the camp were answered.

1. The children tents are all set up.

 ____

2. The women training includes first aid.

 ____

3. The lifeguards attention stays on the swimmers.

 ____

4. The geese water is changed often.

 ____

5. The ponies saddles fit securely.

 ____

6. The campers days go by quickly.

 ____

Present Tense

Verbs show more than the action in a sentence. They also tell when the action happens.

Lisa **opens** the door.

The verb *opens* tells that Lisa is opening the door now. A verb that tells what its subject is doing right now is in the **present tense**. Notice that *s* has been added to *open*. You change the form of a verb to show the present tense when a singular noun is the subject.

You do not change the form of verbs when they are used with plural subjects or with *I* or *you*.

The twins **smile**. I **smile**. You **smile**.

Rules for Forming the Present Tense	
1. Most verbs: Add *-s*.	hold — hold**s** cut — cut**s**
2. Verbs ending in *s*, *ch*, *sh*, *x*, and *z*: Add *-es*.	miss — miss**es** match — match**es** wash — wash**es** fix — fix**es** buzz — buzz**es**
3. Verbs ending with a consonant and *y*: Change the *y* to *i* and add *-es*.	fly — fl**ies** hurry — hurr**ies**

Guided Practice

Which present tense form of the verb in parentheses is correct?

Example: The car ______. (pass) *(passes)*

1. Mom ______. (watch)
2. The girls ______. (push)
3. The key ______. (drop)
4. The shirt ______. (dry)
5. They ______. (sing)
6. The drink ______. (fizz)

REMINDER

- A **present tense verb** shows action that happens now.
- Add *-s* or *-es* to most verbs to show the present tense if the subject is singular.

  She **runs**. Ramon **waxes** his skis.
  He **plays**. She **brushes** her teeth.
  Pat **washes** her hands. One fly **buzzes**.
  The thunder **crashes**. The baby **cries**.
- Do not add *-s* or *-es* if the subject is plural or *I* or *you*.

  I **bake**. They **mix**.
  You **play**. The babies **cry**.

INDEPENDENT PRACTICE

Rewrite each sentence, using the correct verb in parentheses.

Example: Mr. Tsao (fixes, fix) bikes.
Mr. Tsao fixes bikes.

1. Sometimes riders (crash, crashes) their bikes.

____

2. I (like, likes) to work for Mr. Tsao.

____

3. He (teach, teaches) me after school.

____

4. I (watches, watch) what Mr. Tsao does.

____

5. He (patches, patch) tires that are flat.

____

6. He (try, tries) to make the bikes as good as new.

____

7. We (wash, washes) the bikes for the customers.

____

8. People happily (pays, pay) their bills.

____

Past Tense

You have learned that verbs in the present tense show what is happening. A verb that shows what has already happened is in the **past tense**.

CHOP P ED

My brother **worked** in a flower shop.

The verb *worked* is in the past tense. It tells that the action in the sentence happened before now.

There are several ways to form the past tense. You must look at the ending of a verb to see how to form its past tense.

Rules for Forming the Past Tense	
1. Most verbs: Add *-ed.*	spray — spray**ed** screech — screech**ed**
2. Verbs ending with *e:* Add *-d.*	arrive — arriv**ed** file — fil**ed**
3. Verbs ending with a consonant and *y:* Change the *y* to *i* and add *-ed.*	worry — worr**ied** study — stud**ied**
4. Verbs ending with a single vowel and a consonant: Double the final consonant and add *-ed.*	wrap — wrap**ped** grab — grab**bed**

GUIDED PRACTICE

What is the past tense of each verb?

Example: miss *missed*

1. hurry
2. sew
3. hatch
4. mend
5. pull
6. glue
7. jog
8. handle
9. slip
10. rake
11. marry
12. obey
13. slice
14. stun

REMINDER

- A **past tense verb** shows that something already happened.
- Form the past tense of most verbs by adding *-ed.*

Present Tense	Past Tense
Now we pack.	Last week we **packed**.
Now we move.	Last week we **moved**.
Now we reply.	Last week we **replied**.
Now we play.	Last week we **played**.
Now we trot.	Last week we **trotted**.

INDEPENDENT PRACTICE

Use the past tense form of the verb in parentheses to complete each sentence. Write the sentence correctly.

Example: Once my sister __?__ a flower shop. **(own)**
Once my sister owned a flower shop.

1. She __?__ there for three years. **(work)**

2. People outside often __?__ at her. **(wave)**

3. Once a customer __?__ a green plant. **(admire)**

4. The man __?__ the tiny leaves. **(touch)**

5. The leaves immediately __?__ up. **(curl)**

6. The customer __?__ to look calm. **(try)**

7. My sister __?__ at his reaction. **(grin)**

8. She __?__ the plant's response to touch. **(explain)**

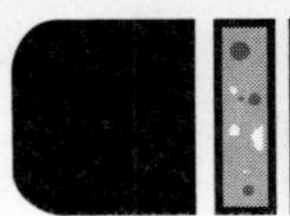

Future Tense

You know that verbs can tell what is happening now or what has happened in the past. A verb that tells what is going to happen is in the **future tense**.

> Holly **will take** a trip next month.
> Holly and Kona **will travel** across the country.

To form the future tense of a verb, use the helping verb *will* or *shall* with the main verb.

> **Shall** I call Holly?
> We **will** probably see them after the trip.

GUIDED PRACTICE

A. What is the future tense form of each verb?

Example: attend *will attend*

1.	creep	**3.**	build	**5.**	pay	**7.**	perform
2.	live	**4.**	grow	**6.**	thank	**8.**	sparkle

B. What is the future tense form of each underlined verb?

Example: My cousins drive to Texas. *will drive*

9. They stop in Tyler.
10. Visitors attend a festival there.
11. Large crowds visit the Rose Bowl Chili Cook-Off.
12. Several good cooks serve hot bowls of chili.
13. Then my cousins travel to Hereford.
14. Signs announce the National Cowgirl Hall of Fame.
15. Cowgirls love that place.

Reminder

- A **future tense verb** tells what is going to happen.
- Use the main verb with the helping verb *will* or *shall* to form the future tense.

We **shall tell** them about San Antonio.
They **will enjoy** that city.

Independent Practice

Write each sentence. Use the future tense form of the verb in parentheses.

Example: Holly and Kona (go, will go) to the Tower of the Americas.
Holly and Kona will go to the Tower of the Americas.

1. They (will climb, climb) very high.

____

2. Guides (explained, will explain) the history of the city.

____

3. My cousins (walk, will walk) along the San Antonio River.

____

4. Kona (will enter, enters) the colorful shops.

____

5. Holly (will ride, rides) a boat along the river.

____

6. They (will enjoy, enjoy) the beauty of the river.

____

7. They (noticed, will notice) the old Spanish buildings.

____

8. They (come, will come) back to the city.

____

Subject–Verb Agreement

A present tense verb and its subject must **agree** in number. If the subject is singular, use the singular form of the verb. If the subject is plural, use the plural form of the verb. Study the rules for subject–verb agreement in the chart below.

SINGULAR: A **kangaroo hops** on its hind legs.
PLURAL: **Kangaroos live** in Australia.

Rules for Subject–Verb Agreement	
1. **Singular subject:** Add *-s* or *-es* to the verb.	**Fur covers** a kangaroo's body. The **animal eats** plants. **It searches** for food at night.
2. **Plural subject:** Do not add *-s* or *-es* to the verb.	The **tails grow** to three feet. The **tail and legs support** it. **They balance** the animal.
3. **I or you:** Use the plural form of the verb.	**I like** the babies. **You see** them in pouches.

Look at the second example for Rule 2. The compound subject *tail and legs* is followed by the plural form of the verb. When the parts of a compound subject are joined by *and*, always use the plural form of the verb.

Guided Practice

Which verb in parentheses correctly completes each sentence?

Example: A kangaroo (move, moves) quickly. *moves*

1. It (run, runs) as fast as forty miles per hour.
2. Speed and balance (help, helps) the animal jump.
3. I (watch, watches) them in films.
4. Kangaroos (fascinate, fascinates) me.
5. Gary (want, wants) more information about them.

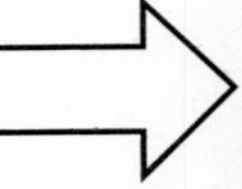

REMINDER

- A present tense verb and its subject must **agree** in number.

Singular Subjects	**Plural Subjects**	***I* or *you***
A man **arrives**.	Two people **arrive**.	I **arrive**.
He **looks** inside.	They **look** inside.	You **look** inside.
A car **stops**.	Cars and bikes **stop**.	I **stop**.

INDEPENDENT PRACTICE

Write the correct verb in parentheses to complete each sentence.

Example: My brother and I __see__ the kangaroos. **(see, sees)**

1. We ____________ the adults. **(watch, watches)**
2. One female ____________ closer. **(come, comes)**
3. Her baby ____________ from us. **(hide, hides)**
4. The mother ____________ it in her pouch. **(keep, keeps)**
5. It ____________ there for six months. **(live, lives)**
6. Pouches ____________ warmth. **(offer, offers)**
7. Young kangaroos ____________ protection. **(need, needs)**
8. They ____________ without it. **(die, dies)**
9. An older baby ____________ nearby. **(hop, hops)**
10. It ____________ outside the pouch. **(survive, survives)**
11. Two babies ____________ the same mother. **(share, shares)**
12. You ____________ only the older one. **(see, sees)**
13. The keeper ____________ the baby a joey. **(call, calls)**
14. She ____________ us a life-sized picture. **(show, shows)**
15. It ____________ bald to me! **(look, looks)**
16. I ____________ my brother a ruler. **(give, gives)**
17. He ____________ the picture of the joey. **(measure, measures)**
18. My brother and I ____________ that it is one inch tall! **(doubt, doubts)**

Agreement with be and have

You must change the forms of the verbs *be* and *have* in special ways to agree with their subjects. The chart below shows the past and present tense forms.

Subject	Form of *be*	Form of *have*
Singular subjects:		
I	am, was	have, had
You	are, were	have, had
He, she, it (or singular noun)	is, was	has, had
Plural subjects:		
We	are, were	have, had
You	are, were	have, had
They (or plural noun)	are, were	have, had

GUIDED PRACTICE

Which form of *be* or *have* in parentheses correctly completes each sentence?

Example: Bonnie (is, are) interested in butterflies. *is*

1. We (was, were) impressed by her knowledge.
2. She (has, have) read a lot about butterflies.
3. I (has, have) listened to her.
4. Butterflies (is, are) beautiful insects.
5. They (is, are) every color of the rainbow.
6. (Has, Have) you seen any this year?
7. They (is, are) very common in summer.
8. Jeff (has, have) some posters of butterflies.
9. Gill and Debbie (has, have) seen yellow ones.
10. Jeff (is, are) looking for other colors.

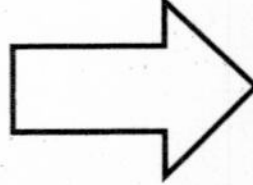

REMINDER

- The verbs *be* and *have* have different forms. Use the form that agrees with the subject of the sentence.

Subjects	**Forms of *be***	**Forms of *have***
I	am, was	have, had
he, she, it	is, was	has, had
singular nouns	is, was	has, had
you, we, they	are, were	have, had
plural nouns	are, were	have, had

INDEPENDENT PRACTICE

Write each sentence correctly. Use the verb in parentheses that agrees with the subject.

Example: Moths (is, are) different from butterflies.

Moths are different from butterflies.

1. Bonnie (was, were) explaining the differences.

____

2. She (has, have) some pictures.

____

3. In one picture, a moth (is, are) at rest.

____

4. It (has, have) stretched its wings out flat.

____

5. Butterflies (is, are) resting in another picture.

____

6. They (has, have) their wings straight up.

____

7. We (has, have) asked Bonnie about other differences.

____

8. Gill and I (is, are) trying to learn more.

____

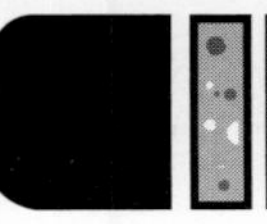

Regular and Irregular Verbs

You have learned to form the past tense and to use helping verbs to show that something has already happened. For most verbs, you form the past by adding *-d* or *-ed* to the verb. Verbs that follow this rule are called **regular verbs**.

march — marched smile — smiled fry — fried

For some verbs, you do not form the past by adding *-d* or *-ed*. **Irregular verbs** have special forms to show the past.

Irregular Verbs

Verb	Past tense	Past with helping verb
bring	brought	(has, have, had) brought
come	came	(has, have, had) come
go	went	(has, have, had) gone
make	made	(has, have, had) made
run	ran	(has, have, had) run
say	said	(has, have, had) said
take	took	(has, have, had) taken
think	thought	(has, have, had) thought
write	wrote	(has, have, had) written

GUIDED PRACTICE

A. Which of these past tense verbs are regular? Which are irregular?

Example: gone *irregular*

1. melted
2. brought
3. said
4. denied
5. came
6. made
7. helped
8. wrote

B. What is the past form of each verb above when it is used with a helping verb?

Example: go *have gone*

Reminder

- Add *-d* or *-ed* to **regular verbs** to show the past.
- **Irregular verbs** have special forms to show the past.

	Verb	**Past Tense**	**Past with Helping Verb**
Regular Verbs:	walk	walked	(has, have, had) walked
	hope	hoped	(has, have, had) hoped
	dry	dried	(has, have, had) dried
Irregular Verbs:	come	came	(has, have, had) come
	think	thought	(has, have, had) thought

Independent Practice

Look at each underlined verb or verb phrase. Label it *regular* or *irregular.*

Example: Ana liked my pet rabbits. **regular**

1. She came one day to see them. ________
2. She stayed a long time. ________
3. I have made a hobby of rabbits. ________
4. I shared my books about rabbits. ________
5. Ana thought that the pictures were wonderful. ________
6. She took a book home to read. ________
7. Ana has brought the book back. ________
8. She has written a list of her favorites. ________
9. Ana had enjoyed some of their names. ________
10. She had laughed at the name Swiss Fox. ________
11. She had thought Ham Blue was funny too. ________
12. Last week we went to a rabbit show. ________
13. We tried to see a Ham Blue. ________
14. Both of us had wondered how blue it really was. ________
15. We almost ran from booth to booth. ________
16. We made people smile at all our questions. ________

Proper Adjectives

An adjective formed from a proper noun is called a **proper adjective**. Like a proper noun, a proper adjective is capitalized.

PROPER NOUN: This recipe is from **Austria**.
PROPER ADJECTIVE: It is an **Austrian** recipe.

Proper noun	Proper adjective
Canada	**Canadian** customs
China	**Chinese** food
Switzerland	**Swiss** clock
Costa Rica	**Costa Rican** history

Notice that the proper adjective *Costa Rican* is two words that describe one thing. When a proper adjective is two words, capitalize both words.

GUIDED PRACTICE

How would you form a proper adjective from the underlined noun to complete each sentence? Use your dictionary if you need help.

Example: Stew made in Ireland is ______________ stew. *Irish*

1. Bread from Italy is ______________ bread.

2. Bakers in Denmark make ______________ pastries.

3. Rice from Turkey is ______________ rice.

4. Thick waffles from Belgium are ______________ waffles.

5. Use olives from Greece for a ______________ salad.

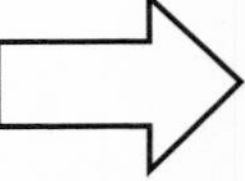

REMINDER

- A **proper adjective** is formed from a proper noun.
- A proper adjective begins with a capital letter.

The meal begins with a **Korean** meat salad.
Then we eat a **West Indian** fish soup.
The **Swedish** dessert looks delicious.

INDEPENDENT PRACTICE

Underline the proper adjective in each sentence. Then write it correctly.

Example: The canadian pea soup is yellow. **Canadian**

1. I have tasted the japanese bean soup. ________
2. This russian soup was made from beets. ________
3. Will you try the north african rice? ________
4. The english lamb chop looks very thick. ________
5. The hungarian stew is full of vitamins. ________
6. The bread is a flat indian bread. ________
7. I will also try the dark polish bread. ________
8. Put some of that french cheese on it. ________
9. What is the name of the spanish rice dish? ________
10. Please pass the swiss potatoes. ________
11. That mexican corn is wonderful! ________
12. Try some of these indonesian pickles. ________
13. This greek salad has cheese in it. ________
14. Use chopsticks for the chinese vegetables. ________
15. The bananas are a south american dessert. ________
16. Try the dutch dessert made from yogurt. ________
17. Many armenian desserts are sweetened with honey. ________
18. Rayna's favorite is the puerto rican egg custard. ________

Comparing with good and bad

The adjectives *good* and *bad* have special forms for making comparisons. These words do not take the endings *-er* and *-est* or use the words *more* and *most* to make comparisons.

GOOD: Today the weather was **good**.
Yesterday it was even **better**.
Tomorrow will be the **best** day of all.

BAD: A **bad** hurricane struck last month.
The storm last year was **worse**.
The **worst** hurricane hit in 1938.

Comparing with *good* and *bad*		
Describing one person, place, or thing	good	bad
Comparing two persons, places, or things	better	worse
Comparing three or more persons, places, or things	best	worst

GUIDED PRACTICE

What is the correct form of *good* or *bad* in each sentence?

Example: A hurricane is a (bad, worst) tropical storm. *bad*

1. The (worse, worst) hurricanes of all often hit in the fall.
2. Today we have (good, best) ways to forecast them.
3. Of all the methods, radar is the (better, best).
4. It gives a very (good, better) warning.
5. The (bad, worst) damage of all happens when people are not ready.
6. That is why the last storm was (worse, worst) than this one.
7. Now we do a (better, best) job of preparing for storms.
8. We learned our lesson from that (bad, worse) storm last fall.

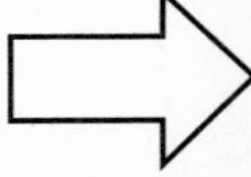

Reminder

- The adjectives *good* and *bad* have special forms for making comparisons.
- Use *better* and *worse* to compare two.
- Use *best* and *worst* to compare three or more.

Good: Weather forecasters keep **good** records.
The records are **better** now than last year.
Accurate forecasts are our **best** protection.

Bad: Hurricanes are **bad** storms.
They are **worse** than blizzards.
Winds over 150 miles per hour do the **worst** damage.

Independent Practice

Rewrite each sentence, using the correct adjective in parentheses.

Example: The (worse, worst) damage of all comes from wind and water.
The worst damage comes from wind and water.

1. A (good, best) plan is important for protection.

____

2. High waves cause very (bad, worst) floods along coastlines.

____

3. Flooding is (worse, worst) on open coastlines than on protected ones.

____

4. High tide is the (worse, worst) time of all for a storm.

____

5. It is (better, best) for people to leave than to stay.

____

6. Getting to high ground is a very (good, best) idea.

____

7. Of all choices, the (better, best) decision is to go far inland.

____

8. In the (worse, worst) storm, flooding killed six thousand people.

____

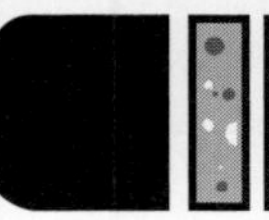

Subject Pronouns

A **pronoun** is a word that takes the place of a noun. A **subject pronoun** takes the place of a noun as the subject of a sentence.

NOUN	SUBJECT PRONOUN
Ruth grooms the horse.	**She** grooms the horse.
A saddle hangs on the wall.	**It** hangs on the wall.
Darcy and Logan ride.	**They** ride.

Subject pronouns also appear after forms of the linking verb *be*. Study the following examples.

Today the best rider is **she**.
Yesterday the best riders were **Steve and I**.

Subject Pronouns	
Singular: I you he, she, it	**Plural:** we you they

GUIDED PRACTICE

A. What are the subject pronouns in these sentences?

Example: She and I like to ride. *She I*

1. They check the saddle.
2. It is perfect now.
3. He rides well.
4. You make nice turns.
5. The best riders are we.
6. The winners are Ruth and I.

B. What subject pronouns could replace the underlined words?

Example: Luiz and Jorge raced. *They*

7. The race was close.
8. Grandmother clapped.
9. David made a jump.
10. He and I landed well.
11. The contest was over.
12. The judge was Kate.

Reminder

- A **pronoun** is a word that replaces a noun.
- The **subject pronouns** are *I, you, he, she, it, we,* and *they.*
- Use subject pronouns as subjects and after forms of the verb *be.*

Nouns	**Subject Pronouns**
Tim and I learn about horses.	**We** learn about horses.
The real expert is Anita.	The real expert is **she**.

Independent Practice

Write the subject pronoun in each sentence.

Example: Did she talk about early horses? ____**she**____

1. They were only two feet tall. ____________
2. Claire and I were surprised. ____________
3. The most surprised person was she. ____________
4. Do you know about the early horse? ____________
5. At some point, it became a large animal. ____________
6. We learned about the Greeks and Romans. ____________
7. They trained horses for war. ____________
8. Tim and I have seen pictures of chariots. ____________
9. The students most interested in this history were we. ____________
10. It is a very long history! ____________
11. I also learned something about Columbus. ____________
12. He had horses on the second voyage. ____________
13. Did he come before the Spanish settlers? ____________
14. They brought horses to the New World. ____________
15. Will you find out more about horses? ____________
16. It will be difficult to learn more than Anita! ____________

Object Pronouns

You have learned that subject pronouns can replace nouns that are subjects and nouns that follow forms of the linking verb *be*. **Object pronouns** can replace nouns used after action verbs or after words such as *to, for, with, in,* or *at*. The object pronouns are *me, you, him, her, it, us,* and *them*.

NOUN	OBJECT PRONOUN
Ray saw **Mrs. Sykes**.	Ray saw **her**.
Ray asked for **Jon and Suzi**.	Ray asked for **them**.

You and *it* may be subject pronouns or object pronouns.

SUBJECT PRONOUN	OBJECT PRONOUN
You call first.	I called **you** yesterday.
It did not ring.	We will fix **it**.

Be careful not to confuse subject pronouns with object pronouns. Study this chart.

Subject pronouns		**Object pronouns**	
I	we	me	us
you	you	you	you
she, he, it	they	her, him, it	them

GUIDED PRACTICE

Which pronoun in parentheses is correct? Is it a subject pronoun or an object pronoun?

Example: Ray drove (I, me) to my job.
me *object pronoun*

1. Jon took (she, her) on the bus.
2. Suzi and (he, him) baby-sat often.
3. The babies missed (we, us).
4. Jon sang songs to (them, they).
5. Ray thanked Suzi and (he, him) for baby-sitting.

REMINDER

- The **object pronouns** are *me, you, him, her, it, us,* and *them.*
- Use object pronouns after action verbs and words like *to* and *for.*

Nouns	**Object Pronouns**
Mom bought a ticket.	Mom bought **it**.
Mom spoke to Dell and Sara.	Mom spoke to **them**.

- *It* and *you* may be used as subject pronouns or as object pronouns.

subject: **You** can baby-sit for little Mary. object: Mom chose **you**.

INDEPENDENT PRACTICE

Rewrite each sentence correctly, using the object pronoun in parentheses.

Example: Dell told (me, I) some of the rules.

Dell told me some of the rules.

1. Mom and Dad gave (him, he) good advice.

____

2. Dell listened carefully to (they, them).

____

3. Small toys are dangerous for (she, her).

____

4. Mary may put (they, them) in her mouth.

____

5. We should watch (she, her) near the stairs.

____

6. The baby smiles and waves at (we, us).

____

7. Dell pours some juice for Mary and (me, I).

____

8. Mary carries the juice with (she, her) in a bottle.

____

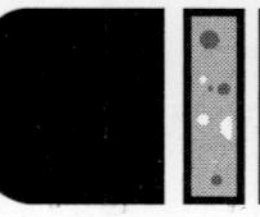

Possessive Pronouns

Possessive nouns show ownership. A **possessive pronoun** can replace a possessive noun. Some possessive pronouns appear before nouns.

Craig's book is old. **His** book is old.

Other possessive pronouns stand alone and replace nouns in a sentence.

The new book is **Afi's**. The new book is **hers**.

Their books are different. **Theirs** are different.

Two Kinds of Possessive Pronouns			
Possessive pronouns used with nouns		**Possessive pronouns that stand alone**	
my	**My** hobby is reading.	**mine**	This hobby is **mine**.
your	Heat **your** soup.	**yours**	**Yours** is cold.
his	**His** house is warm.	**his**	The warm house is **his**.
her	This is **her** shelf.	**hers**	**Hers** is the full shelf.
its	**Its** center is sagging.	**its**	**Its** is the sagging center.
our	**Our** books are heavy.	**ours**	These books are **ours**.
your	Use **your** bookmarks.	**yours**	Place **yours** here.
their	**Their** stories are true.	**theirs**	Those stories are **theirs**.

GUIDED PRACTICE

Which possessive pronoun in parentheses correctly completes each sentence?

Example: Bev and Afi explained (their, theirs) hobbies. *their*

1. (My, Mine) is walking in the woods.
2. Afi displayed (her, hers) collection of buttons.
3. Is that hobby similar to (your, yours)?
4. (Her, Hers) is a very large collection.
5. (Their, Theirs) differences surprised us.
6. The sizes and shapes caught (our, ours) attention.

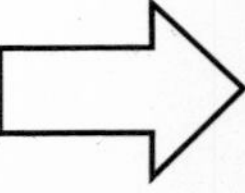

Reminder

- A **possessive pronoun** shows ownership.
- Use *my, your, his, her, its, our,* and *their* before nouns.
- *Mine, yours, his, hers, its, ours,* and *theirs* stand alone and replace nouns in sentences.

Before Nouns	**Stand Alone**
Her friends are here.	The friends are **hers**.
Their stamps are special.	**Theirs** are special.

Independent Practice

Rewrite each sentence, using the correct possessive pronoun in parentheses. The underlined nouns are clues.

Example: Bev's stamp collection is different from (my, mine).
Bev's stamp collection is different from mine.

1. Is this album (your, yours)?

____

2. I bought (my, mine) album at a store.

____

3. Bev made (her, hers) from blue paper.

____

4. All of (her, hers) stamps are blue.

____

5. Are the stamps in (your, yours) album blue?

____

6. (My, Mine) are many colors from one country.

____

7. (Her, Hers) come from different countries.

____

8. Bev's album is not like (our, ours).

____

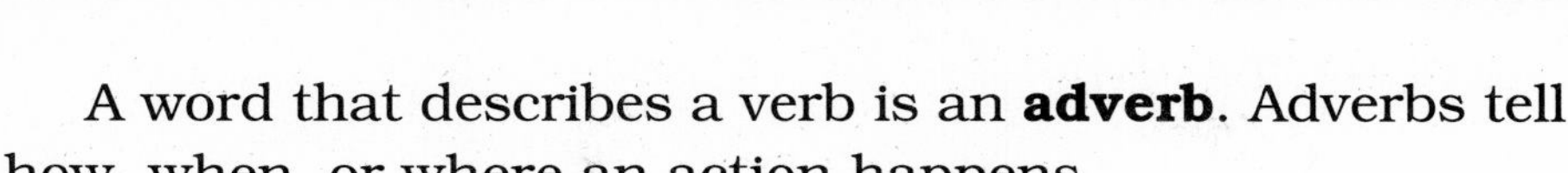

Adverbs

A word that describes a verb is an **adverb**. Adverbs tell how, when, or where an action happens.

HOW: The travelers pushed steadily to the west.

WHEN: Often families faced hardships.

WHERE: They moved their wagons forward.

Many adverbs end with *-ly*. Some are included in these lists of common adverbs.

HOW	WHEN	WHERE
fast	tomorrow	here
hard	later	inside
together	again	far
happily	soon	upstairs
quietly	first	downtown
secretly	next	somewhere
slowly	then	there

Guided Practice

What adverb describes the underlined verb in each sentence? Does it tell how, when, or where?

Example: The settlers went westward. *westward* *where*

1. Some people left early.
2. They slowly crossed the mountains.
3. They journeyed beyond.
4. Eventually, groups settled in the Mississippi Valley.
5. They established many homes there.
6. Men and women bravely started towns.
7. Each family quickly cleared the land.
8. Then they planted many important crops.
9. They rapidly built houses for shelter.
10. Everyone carefully prepared for a harsh winter.

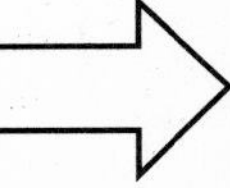

REMINDER

- An **adverb** is a word that tells how, when, or where.
- Adverbs can describe verbs.
- Many adverbs end with *-ly.*

How: Other people followed **continuously**.

When: **Soon** they traveled beyond the valley.

Where: They went **far**.

INDEPENDENT PRACTICE

Write the adverb that describes each underlined verb.

Example: Families later settled in the West. **later**

1. They wisely formed wagon trains. ______
2. Wagons clustered together for safety. ______
3. The journey often lasted five months. ______
4. A leader guided each train forward. ______
5. Most groups followed the Oregon Trail closely. ______
6. There the trail crossed the plains. ______
7. Then it took a mountain route. ______
8. The wagons rolled along. ______
9. They stopped regularly for meals. ______
10. A wagon covered fifteen miles daily. ______
11. The journey tested people thoroughly. ______
12. The hot sun beat down. ______
13. The cold deeply chilled them. ______
14. Sickness followed them everywhere. ______
15. Some finally reached the Pacific Coast. ______
16. Soon their lives became easier. ______

Adjective or Adverb?

Many adverbs are formed by adding *-ly* to adjectives. These words look similar and are easy to confuse. Be careful to use them correctly in a sentence.

INCORRECT: Dad shops **quick**. (adjective)

CORRECT: Dad shops **quickly**. (adverb)

Remember to use an adjective to describe a noun or a pronoun. Use an adverb to describe a verb.

ADJECTIVE: Dad uses easy recipes.

ADVERB: Dad follows them easily.

The words *good* and *well* are also often confused. *Good* is always an adjective. Use *good* before a noun or after a linking verb. Do not use *good* when you mean "healthy."

ADJECTIVE: Choose a good melon. The fruit is good.

Use *well* as an adverb to describe a verb. Use it as an adjective to mean "healthy."

ADVERB: Dad chops the celery well.

ADJECTIVE: Mack is not well enough to cook today.

Guided Practice

Which word in parentheses correctly completes each sentence?

Example: Dad prepares the meal (good, well). *well*

1. He has a (good, well) plan.
2. The frying pan heats (rapid, rapidly).
3. Dad is (careful, carefully) at the stove.
4. He mixes the vegetables (thorough, thoroughly).
5. He whistles a (happy, happily) tune.
6. We thank him (loud, loudly) for the delicious dinner.

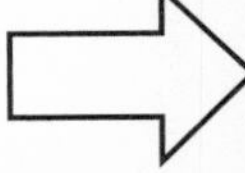

REMINDER

- Use adjectives to describe nouns or pronouns. Use adverbs to describe verbs.
- Do not confuse *good* and *well*. *Good* is always an adjective. *Well* is an adverb unless it means "healthy."

Adjectives	**Adverbs**
My sister is **creative**.	She thinks **creatively**.
Her salads are **good**.	She cooks **well**.
She stays **well**.	She bakes cakes **well**.

INDEPENDENT PRACTICE

Write the word in parentheses that correctly describes the underlined word or words.

Example: Shastin has (good, well) ideas. **good**

1. She bakes (good, well). ______
2. Her recipes are always (unusual, unusually). ______
3. She made a (good, well) cake this week. ______
4. She frosted the cake (careful, carefully). ______
5. Look (close, closely) at the decoration. ______
6. The frosting shows different languages (clear, clearly). ______
7. Each language is (special, specially). ______
8. Shastin spelled each word (correct, correctly). ______
9. She wrote Chinese words (beautiful, beautifully) in one color. ______
10. Spanish words appear in a (different, differently) color. ______
11. Shastin has done her work (good, well). ______
12. Her desserts are (popular, popularly) in our neighborhood. ______

Negatives

Words that mean "no" or "not" are called **negatives**.

Europe has **no** wild lions. There are **none** in Europe.

You have learned to form a contraction from a verb and *not*. These contractions are also negatives. The letters *n't* stand for *not*. The word *not* is an adverb.

Wild lions **don't** live in Europe now.

They **can't** survive there.

Here is a list of some other common negatives.

not	nowhere	nobody	aren't	haven't
never	nothing	no one	doesn't	wouldn't

A sentence should have only one negative. Using double negatives in a sentence is usually incorrect.

INCORRECT	CORRECT
The lion <u>hasn't</u> <u>no</u> space.	The lion **hasn't** any space. The lion **has no** space.
<u>Doesn't</u> <u>nobody</u> care?	**Doesn't** anybody care? Does **nobody** care?
We <u>haven't</u> learned <u>nothing</u>.	We **haven't** learned anything. We have learned **nothing**.

Guided Practice

Which word in parentheses correctly completes each sentence?

Example: Didn't you (ever, never) read about lions? *ever*

1. Doesn't (anybody, nobody) know the history?
2. Europeans haven't seen (any, no) lions for centuries.
3. Lions aren't (anywhere, nowhere) in Australia.
4. They haven't (anywhere, nowhere) to live.
5. No conditions (are, aren't) right outside of Africa.

Reminder

- A **negative** is a word that means "no" or "not."
- Do not use double negatives in a sentence.

Incorrect: **Can't nobody** tell me more?
Correct: **Can't anybody** tell me more?
Can nobody tell me more?

Independent Practice

Write the correct word in parentheses to complete each sentence.

Example: There aren't ____**any**____ wild lions in America. **(any, no)**

1. Haven't you ____________ seen cave drawings? **(ever, never)**
2. Once only two places didn't have ____________ lions. **(no, any)**
3. Today you won't find lions ____________ around you. **(nowhere, anywhere)**
4. There aren't ____________ lions in the Middle East. **(any, no)**
5. Why don't ____________ lions live in those places now? **(any, no)**
6. Doesn't ____________ know the reason? **(nobody, anybody)**
7. No one ____________ sure of the reason? **(isn't, is)**
8. Lions don't live ____________ near cities. **(nowhere, anywhere)**
9. No wild lion ____________ find enough food there. **(can, can't)**
10. Lions don't live freely ____________ except in Africa now. **(nowhere, anywhere)**

Prepositions

Small words that we use all the time can make a big difference in meaning.

I looked **near** the book. I looked **in** the book.

The words *near* and *in* show very different relationships between *looked* and *book*. Words that show relationships between other words are called **prepositions**.

Common Prepositions				
about	before	except	of	through
above	behind	for	off	to
across	below	from	on	under
after	beside	in	out	until
along	by	inside	outside	up
around	down	into	over	with
at	during	near	past	without

A preposition relates some other word in the sentence to the noun or the pronoun that follows the preposition. The noun or the pronoun that follows a preposition is the **object of the preposition**.

I like this book about travel records.

I always carry it with me.

GUIDED PRACTICE

The object of the preposition is underlined in each sentence. What is the preposition?

Example: Travel records are the subject of this book. *of*

1. Someone sailed a small boat around the world.
2. The trip took five hundred days from Australia.
3. A crew crossed the Atlantic in seven days.
4. One man drove a motorboat from England.
5. He took a small boat through a famous canal.

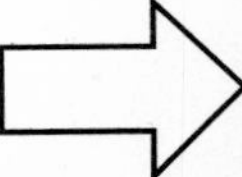

REMINDER

- A **preposition** relates the noun or the pronoun that follows it to another word in the sentence.

  Nellie Bly worked **for** a newspaper.
- The **object of the preposition** is the noun or the pronoun that follows the preposition.

  What kind of **story** did she write?

  She made stories real to her **readers**.

INDEPENDENT PRACTICE

Write the preposition in each sentence. The object of the preposition is underlined to help you.

Example: Nellie Bly read a book about a trip. **about**

1. The book described a trip around the world. ________
2. That trip was completed in eighty days. ________
3. The book gave Bly an idea for a journey. ________
4. She would visit the same places during her trip. ________
5. A large ocean liner took her to the first stop. ________
6. She then crossed the English Channel by ferry. ________
7. A train brought her over mountain passes. ________
8. A steamer carried her down waterways. ________
9. Other ships carried her across oceans. ________
10. She boarded a train on the coast. ________
11. The train brought her into the city. ________
12. Crowds waited inside the station. ________
13. They greeted her with cheers. ________
14. The story covered the front page of her newspaper. ________
15. She had finished the trip in seventy-two days. ________

Prepositional Phrases

You have learned that a preposition is always followed by an object. A **prepositional phrase** is made up of a preposition, the object of the preposition, and all the words between them.

Mice are covered with soft fur.

The object of the preposition can be a compound object.

Some mice live in fields and swamps.

A prepositional phrase can be at the beginning, in the middle, or at the end of a sentence.

Over the years, mice have bothered people.

The people of Rome probably had mice.

Today they are a problem for Dad and Mom.

GUIDED PRACTICE

The preposition is underlined in each sentence. What is the prepositional phrase?

Example: What do you know about the common mouse?
about the common mouse

1. Mice probably came from Asia.
2. Mice spread throughout Europe and the United States.
3. European ships brought them to our shores.
4. They first arrived here in the 1500's.
5. Mice often live inside our homes or barns.
6. They sometimes build nests behind walls.
7. They scamper between the hollow walls.
8. During the day and night, they keep busy.
9. People can hear them at night.
10. Any warm area is a perfect home for a mouse.

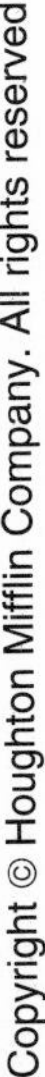

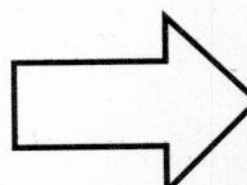

REMINDER

- A **prepositional phrase** is made up of a preposition, its object, and all the words between them.

preposition — object

Mice are happy **with** any human **food**.

prepositional phrase

preposition — object — object

They feast **on** all **grains** and **vegetables**.

prepositional phrase

INDEPENDENT PRACTICE

Underline the prepositional phrase in each sentence. Then write the preposition.

Example: A mouse nests in a dark place. ______ **in** ______

1. The cold drives mice inside a house. ____________
2. During the fall or winter, a mouse needs warmth. ____________
3. Mice line their nests with fabric or straw. ____________
4. They steal feathers from pillows. ____________
5. Through the spring and summer, fields are their homes. ____________
6. Some mice build nests above ceilings. ____________
7. Other mice build them under garage roofs. ____________
8. Mice have enemies in many places. ____________
9. Human beings are the worst enemies of the mouse. ____________
10. They set traps near the nests. ____________
11. They invite cats into their homes and barns. ____________
12. At any moment, a cat can pounce. ____________

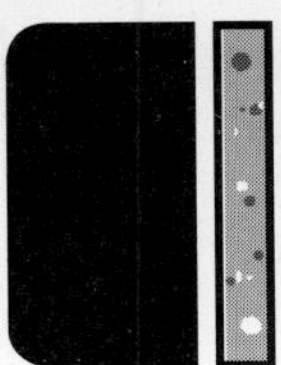

Object Pronouns in Prepositional Phrases

You have learned that the object of a preposition is the noun or the pronoun that follows the preposition. When the object of the preposition is a pronoun, use an object pronoun. Object pronouns are *me, you, him, her, it, us,* and *them*.

People sometimes get confused when the pronoun is part of a compound object. To see whether the pronoun is correct, remove the other object and check the pronoun alone.

My aunt wrote to **Kwesi** and **me**. My aunt wrote to **me**.

Guided Practice

Which pronoun in parentheses correctly completes each sentence?

Example: She planned a trip with Kwesi and (I, me). *me*

1. We traveled to New Orleans with my uncle and (she, her).
2. They rented rooms for my cousins and (us, we).
3. Roy had the room next to Kwesi and (I, me).
4. In the van, Etta sat between Aunt Flo and (he, him).
5. Roy took a tour with Etta and (me, I).
6. I found an interesting walk for (her, she) and my uncle.
7. The boat ride sounded good to Roy and (they, them).
8. Uncle Mel stood beside Aunt Flo and (him, he).
9. The paddle wheel turned above my uncle and (we, us).
10. The waves churned in the water below Kwesi and (she, her).
11. The sun shone brightly above Aunt Flo and (us, we).
12. The Mississippi River flowed behind Kwesi and (I, me).

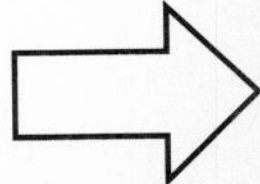

Reminder

- Use object pronouns as objects of prepositions in prepositional phrases.
- Check the pronoun in a compound object by removing the other object.

  Uncle Mel walked beside **Kwesi** and **me**.

  Uncle Mel walked beside **me**.

Independent Practice

Rewrite each sentence, using the correct pronoun in parentheses.

Example: The French Quarter was fun for Roy and (I, me).
The French Quarter was fun for Roy and me.

1. Aunt Flo went shopping without Uncle Mel and (us, we).

2. On Royal Street, we ran ahead of (he, him).

3. I ate at the French Market with Aunt Flo and (them, they).

4. Everyone except Uncle Mel and (she, her) had juice.

5. Aunt Flo ordered coffee for (he, him).

6. Tables of delicious food stood near Kwesi and (me, I).

7. Later I took a walking tour with Uncle Mel and (her, she).

8. New Orleans was a lot of fun for my cousins and (we, us).

CAPITALIZATION, PUNCTUATION, AND USAGE GUIDE

Abbreviations

	Abbreviations are shortened forms of words. Most abbreviations begin with a capital letter and end with a period. Use abbreviations only in special kinds of writing, such as addresses and lists.
Titles	Mr. *(Mister)* Mr. Pedro Arupe Mrs. *(Mistress)* Mrs. Jane Chang Ms. Carla Tower Dr. *(Doctor)* Dr. Ellen Masters Sr. *(Senior)* James Morton, Sr. Jr. *(Junior)* James Morton, Jr. Note: *Miss* is not an abbreviation and does not end with a period.
Words used in addresses	St. *(Street)* Rd. *(Road)* Ave. *(Avenue)* Dr. *(Drive)* Blvd. *(Boulevard)* Rte. *(Route)* Apt. *(Apartment)* Pkwy. *(Parkway)* Mt. *(Mount* or *Mountain)* Expy. *(Expressway)*
Words used in business	Co. *(Company)* Corp. *(Corporation)* Inc. *(Incorporated)* Ltd. *(Limited)*
Other abbreviations	**Some abbreviations are written in all capital letters, with a letter standing for each important word.** P.D. *(Police Department)* J.P. *(Justice of the Peace)* P.O. *(Post Office)* R.N. *(Registered Nurse)*
	The United States Postal Service uses two capital letters and no period in each of its state abbreviations. AL *(Alabama)* AK *(Alaska)* AZ *(Arizona)* AR *(Arkansas)* CA *(California)* CO *(Colorado)* CT *(Connecticut)* DE *(Delaware)* FL *(Florida)* GA *(Georgia)* HI *(Hawaii)* ID *(Idaho)* IL *(Illinois)* IN *(Indiana)* IA *(Iowa)* KS *(Kansas)* KY *(Kentucky)* LA *(Louisiana)* ME *(Maine)* MD *(Maryland)* MA *(Massachusetts)* MI *(Michigan)* MN *(Minnesota)* MS *(Mississippi)* MO *(Missouri)* MT *(Montana)* NE *(Nebraska)* NV *(Nevada)* NH *(New Hampshire)* NJ *(New Jersey)* NM *(New Mexico)* NY *(New York)* NC *(North Carolina)* ND *(North Dakota)* OH *(Ohio)* OK *(Oklahoma)*

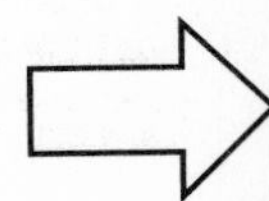

OR *(Oregon)*	TN *(Tennessee)*	WA *(Washington)*
PA *(Pennsylvania)*	TX *(Texas)*	WV *(West Virginia)*
RI *(Rhode Island)*	UT *(Utah)*	WI *(Wisconsin)*
SC *(South Carolina)*	VT *(Vermont)*	WY *(Wyoming)*
SD *(South Dakota)*	VA *(Virginia)*	

Initials are abbreviations that stand for a person's first or middle name. Some names have both a first and a middle initial.

T. S. Eliot *(Thomas Stearns Eliot)*
A. Vincent Denning *(Andrew Vincent Denning)*
Mr. Frank D. Ryan *(Mister Frank Donald Ryan)*

Titles

Underlining

The important words and the first and last words in a title are capitalized. Titles of books, magazines, TV shows, movies, and newspapers are underlined.

The Borrowers *(book)*
Yankee *(magazine)*
Sesame Street *(TV show)*
Home Alone *(movie)*
The Baltimore Sun *(newspaper)*

Quotation marks with titles

Titles of short stories, songs, articles, book chapters, and most poems are set off by quotation marks.

"The Ransom of Red Chief" *(short story)*
"Don't Fence Me In" *(song)*
"My Flight in Space" *(article)*
"The World of Plants" *(chapter)*
"Mending Wall" *(poem)*

Quotations

Quotation marks with commas and periods

Quotation marks are used to set off a speaker's exact words. The first word of a quotation begins with a capital letter. Punctuation belongs *inside* the closing quotation marks. Commas separate a quotation from the rest of the sentence.

"When," asked the man, "does the train leave?"
"Please put your bags on the rack," said Ms. Enos.
Gina asked, "When do we eat?"
"Now is the time," answered Kofi. "I'm starved!"

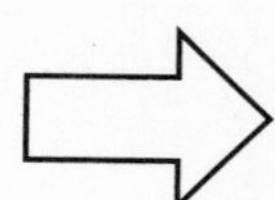

CAPITALIZATION, PUNCTUATION, USAGE

Rules for capitalization

Capitalize the first word of every sentence.
What a lively dog this puppy is!

Capitalize the pronoun I.
When should I leave for school?

Capitalize proper nouns. If a proper noun is made up of more than one word, capitalize each important word.
Clara F. Romero New Mexico Statue of Liberty

Capitalize titles or their abbreviations when used with a person's name.
Captain Wright Representative Hughes Dr. Diaz

Capitalize proper adjectives.
I bought an Australian sweater.
Nora is Polish.
This is a French Canadian dance.

Capitalize the names of days, months, and holidays.
School starts on the first Thursday of September.
We watched the parade on Memorial Day.

Capitalize the names of buildings and companies.
World Trade Center
Benjamin Banneker School
Acme Biscuit Company

Capitalize the first, last, and all important words in a title. Do not capitalize words such as *a, in, and, of,* and *the* unless they begin or end a title.
The Trumpet of the Swan "Up a Road Slowly"
The St. Louis Dispatch "Cowboy Song"

Capitalize the first word of each main topic and subtopic in an outline.
I. Types of storms
 A. Hurricanes
 B. Tornadoes

Capitalize the first word in the greeting and the closing of a letter.
Dear Sandra, Sincerely yours,

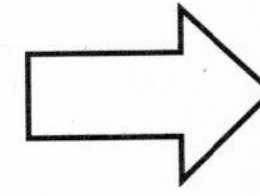

Punctuation

End marks	**There are three end marks. A *period* (.) ends a declarative or imperative sentence. A *question mark* (?) follows an interrogative sentence. An *exclamation point* (!) follows an exclamatory sentence.** The pins are in the drawer. *(declarative)* Check the temperature in the house. *(imperative)* How was this road built? *(interrogative)* This is the biggest fish ever! *(exclamatory)*
Apostrophe	**To form the possessive of a singular noun, add an apostrophe and *s*.** pilot's — grandson's contractor's — relative's
	For a plural noun that ends in *s*, add only an apostrophe. daughters' — crows' families' — hunting dogs'
	For a plural noun that does not end in *s*, add an apostrophe and *s* to form the plural possessive. men's — oxen's mice's — geese's
	Use an apostrophe in contractions in place of dropped letters. Do not use contractions in formal writing. isn't *(is not)* — they're *(they are)* — you'll *(you will)* can't *(cannot)* — it's *(it is)* — could've *(could have)* won't *(will not)* — I'm *(I am)* — would've *(would have)* wasn't *(was not)* — we've *(we have)* — should've *(should have)*
Colon	**Use a colon after the greeting in a business letter.** Dear Ms. Goss: — Dear Anderson's Market:
Comma	**A comma tells your reader where to pause. For words in a series, put a comma after each item except the last. Do not use a comma if only two items are listed.** The girls planted beans, peas, and lettuce.
	Use commas to separate two or more adjectives that are listed together unless one adjective tells how many. A thick, soupy fog rolled across the bay. Two red lights flashed in the dark.
	Use a comma before the conjunction in a compound sentence. The day was warm, but the lake was cold.

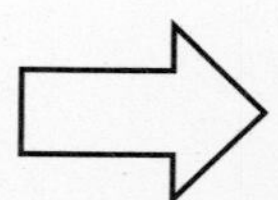

Comma (continued)	**Use commas after introductory words such as *yes, no, oh,* and *well* when they begin a sentence.** Yes, the days are getting shorter. Well, I'll help you.
	Use a comma to separate a noun in direct address. Azi, help me clean the store. Are you done, Jo? Do you know, Pepe, where Dayton is?
	Use a comma between the names of a city and a state. Madison, Wisconsin Jackson, Mississippi
	Use a comma after the greeting in a friendly letter. Dear Crystal, Dear Uncle David,
	Use a comma after the closing in a letter. Your niece, Yours truly,

Problem Words

Words	Rules	Examples
a, an, the	**These words are articles.**	
a, an	**Use *a* and *an* before singular nouns. Use *a* before a word that begins with a consonant sound. Use *an* before a word that begins with a vowel sound.**	a continent an island
the	**Use *the* with both singular and plural nouns. Use *the* to point out particular persons, places, or things.**	the island the islands The shows that I enjoy are comedies.
can	***Can* means "to be able to do something."**	Marta can skate well.
may	***May* means "to be allowed or permitted."**	May I go with you?

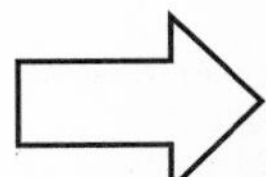

CAPITALIZATION, PUNCTUATION, USAGE

Problem Words continued

Words	Rules	Examples
good	***Good* is an adjective.**	This apple tastes good.
well	***Well* is usually an adverb. It is an adjective only when it refers to health.**	Sara runs well. Does she feel well?
its	***Its* is a possessive pronoun.**	The cat licked its fur.
it's	***It's* is a contraction of *it is*.**	It's clear today.
let	***Let* means "to permit or allow."**	Please let me help you.
leave	***Leave* means "to go away from" or "to let remain in a place."**	The ferry leaves at noon. Leave it on the stove.
sit	***Sit* means "to rest in one place."**	Please sit by the fire.
set	***Set* means "to place or put."**	Set the package on the seat.
teach	***Teach* means "to give instruction."**	He teaches us how to draw.
learn	***Learn* means "to receive instruction."**	We learned a new song.
their	***Their* is a possessive pronoun.**	Their beds are made.
there	***There* is an adverb. It may also begin a sentence.**	Is the boat there? There is the lighthouse.
they're	***They're* is a contraction of *they are*.**	They're willing to help.
two	***Two* is a number.**	We drove two miles.
to	***To* means "in the direction of."**	The train goes to Ames.
too	***Too* means "more than enough" and "also."**	This job is too hard. Can we play too?
your	***Your* is a possessive pronoun.**	Was this your idea?
you're	***You're* is a contraction for *you are*.**	You're our fastest runner.

Adjective and Adverb Usage

Adjective or adverb?	**Use adjectives to describe nouns or pronouns. Use adverbs to describe verbs.** It was a wonderful concert. *(adjective)* She played wonderfully. *(adverb)*
Comparing	**To compare two things or actions, add *-er* to adjectives and adverbs or use the word *more.*** This engine is quieter than that one. It runs more smoothly.
	To compare three or more things or actions, add *-est* or use the word *most.* This engine is the quietest of all three. It runs most smoothly.
	Use *more* or *most* with an adjective or adverb that has two or more syllables, such as *careful* or *politely.* Do not add *-er* or *-est* to long adjectives or adverbs. comfortable — more comfortable — most comfortable rapidly — more rapidly — most rapidly
good, bad	**The adjectives *good* and *bad* have special forms for making comparisons.** good — better — best bad — worse — worst

Negatives

A negative is a word that means "no" or "not." Do not use double negatives in a sentence.

INCORRECT: We didn't bother nobody.
CORRECT: We didn't bother anybody.

Pronoun Usage

Agreement	**A pronoun must agree with the noun to which it refers.** Dad bought fresh peaches. The family ate them. Jan sat at the piano. She played softly.
Double subjects	**Do not use a double subject — a noun and a pronoun — to name the same person, place, or thing.** **INCORRECT:** The climb it was difficult. **CORRECT:** The climb was difficult.

CAPITALIZATION, PUNCTUATION, USAGE

I, me

Use *I* as the subject of a sentence and after forms of *be*. Use *me* after action verbs or prepositions like *to*, *in*, and *for*. (See *Subject and object pronouns*.)

Mali and I swim every afternoon.
She is teaching me.
Will you go with me?

When using *I* or *me* with nouns or other pronouns, always name yourself last.

Sharon and I will remember.
Hold a place in line for Salim and me.

Possessive pronouns

A possessive pronoun shows ownership. Use *my*, *your*, *his*, *her*, *its*, *our*, and *their* before nouns.

My brother is working at their house.

Use *mine*, *yours*, *his*, *hers*, *its*, *ours*, and *theirs* to replace nouns in a sentence.

Yours is helping too.

Subject and object pronouns

Use subject pronouns as subjects and after forms of the verb *be*.

She won many awards for volleyball.
I am he.
The best players are they.

Use object pronouns after action verbs and prepositions like *to* and *for*.

Craig drew pictures and painted them. *(direct object)*
Let's buy this scarf for her. *(object of preposition)*

Compound subjects, compound objects

To decide which pronoun to use in a compound subject or a compound object, leave out the other part of the compound. Say the sentence with the pronoun alone.

Jon and ___________ hike the trails. (*they, them*)
They hike the trails.
Jon and they hike the trails.
I helped Mom and ___________. *(she, her)*
I helped her.
I helped Mom and her.
Aunt Harriet wrote to Phil and ___________. *(I, me)*
Aunt Harriet wrote to me.
Aunt Harriet wrote to Phil and me.

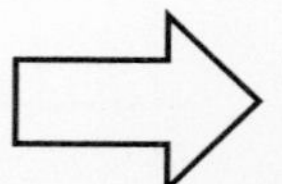

***We* and *us* with nouns**	**Use *we* with a noun that is a subject or that follows a linking verb.** **INCORRECT:** Us students took the test. **CORRECT:** We students took the test. **INCORRECT:** The champions are us girls. **CORRECT:** The champions are we girls.
	Use *us* with a noun that follows an action verb or that follows a preposition such as *to, for, with,* or *at.* **INCORRECT:** Mr. Abrams coached we runners. **CORRECT:** Mr. Abrams coached us runners. **INCORRECT:** He worked with we sprinters. **CORRECT:** He worked with us sprinters.

Verb Usage

Agreement: subject–verb	**A present tense verb and its subject must agree in number. Add *-s* or *-es* to the verb if the subject is singular. Do not add *-s* or *-es* to the verb if the subject is plural or if the subject is *I*.** Mr. Salinas knows my cousin. She rushes to help. The days seem long. I enjoy walking.
	Change the forms of *be* and *have* to make them agree with their subjects. She is weeding the garden now. Have they left home yet? They are walking quickly. Jason has a busy schedule.
Agreement: compound subjects	**A compound subject with *and* takes a plural verb.** Del, Paula, and Lu have new jackets.
could have, should have	**Use *could have, would have, should have, might have, must have.* Avoid using *of* with *could, would, should, might,* or *must*.** He could have (*not* could of) run faster. Kita would have (*not* would of) enjoyed the trip. They should have (*not* should of) left earlier. You might have (*not* might of) won a prize. She must have (*not* must of) set a new record.

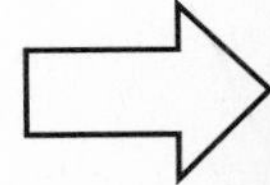

Irregular verbs

Irregular verbs do not add *-ed* or *-d* to form the past tense. Because irregular verbs do not follow a regular pattern, you must memorize their spellings. Use *has, have,* or *had* as a helping verb with the past tense.

Verb	**Past**	**Past with helping verb**
be	was	been
begin	began	begun
blow	blew	blown
break	broke	broken
bring	brought	brought
choose	chose	chosen
come	came	come
fly	flew	flown
freeze	froze	frozen
go	went	gone
grow	grew	grown
have	had	had
know	knew	known
make	made	made
ring	rang	rung
run	ran	run
say	said	said
sing	sang	sung
speak	spoke	spoken
steal	stole	stolen
swim	swam	swum
take	took	taken
tear	tore	torn
think	thought	thought
wear	wore	worn
write	wrote	written

My Notes

My Notes